The Sociology of Food:
Eating, Diet and Culture

DATE DUE

The Sociology of Food:
Eating, Diet and Culture

Stephen Mennell
Anne Murcott
Anneke H. van Otterloo

SAGE Publications
London · Newbury Park · New Delhi

First published 1992, Reprinted 1993

SAGE Publications Ltd
6 Bonhill Street
London EC2A 4PU

SAGE Publications Inc
2455 Teller Road
Newbury Park, California 91320

SAGE Publications India Pvt Ltd
32, M-Block Market
Greater Kailash – I
New Delhi 110 048

British Library Cataloguing in Publication Data

Mennell, Stephen
  Sociology of Food: Eating, Diet and Culture
  I. Title
  394.12
  ISBN 0-8039-8839-7
  ISBN 0-8039-8838-9 pbk

Library of Congress catalog card number 92-050680

Printed in Great Britain by J.W. Arrowsmith Ltd., Bristol

Contents

Acknowledgements

We should like to thank Katie Purvis for her assistance in searching bibliographies for this report, the Research Committee of the Faculty of Arts, Monash University, for a research grant which made that possible, and Liz Walford and Jill Bourne for similar assistance supported by the School of Social & Administrative Studies, University of Wales College of Cardiff. We are also grateful to Dr Katherine Simons for her collaboration in writing Part 6 of this report and to Virginia Olesen and Ritva Prättälä for drawing our attention to newly published material.

About the Authors

Stephen Mennell has been Professor of Sociology and Head of the Department of Anthropology and Sociology, Monash University (Clayton [Melbourne] Victoria 3168) Australia, since 1990. Before that he taught for over twenty years at the University of Exeter, in the United Kingdom. His books include *All Manners of Food* (1985) and *Norbert Elias: Civilisation and the Human Self-Image* (1989).

Anne Murcott is Senior Lecturer in Medical Anthropology, Health Promotion Sciences Unit, Department of Public Health & Policy at the London School of Hygiene and Tropical Medicine (Keppel Street, London WC1E 7HT) UK. Before moving there in 1991, she taught sociology for nearly twenty years, in the University of Wales College of Cardiff and University of Wales College of Medicine. Her publications incluce *The Sociology of Food and Eating* (1983, Aldershot: Gower) an edited collection of specially commissioned essays. She is former editor of *Sociology of Health & Illness*, an international journal of medical sociology, and also research coordinator for the Economic and Social Science Research Council's six-year programme 'The Nation's Diet: The Social Science of Food Choice'.

Anneke van Otterloo lectures at the Sociologisch Instituut, University of Amsterdam (Oude Hoogstraat 24, 1012 CE Amsterdam), The Netherlands. Her book *Eten en eetlust in Nederland, 1840–1990* was published in 1990.

Introduction: Significance and Theoretical Orientations

Until quite recently, few sociologists have given much attention to food and eating as topics of serious intellectual interest. Perhaps the sheer biological necessity for human beings to take in nutrients at regular intervals, and even the importance of meals and commensality in the social life of most human societies, were so obvious that they were simply taken for granted – part of the background of 'what everyone knows' already. That sociologists have traditionally studied mainly their own societies – chiefly of the 'advanced industrial' type – has perhaps helped to depress their curiosity about what people eat, how they cook it and eat it, how they feel about it, and why. Another reason may be that food has long belonged to the domestic sphere, formed part of women's work, and thus seemed of lower status than the public spheres of the economy and polity; sociology's search for respectability in the academy was perhaps for a long time unlikely to be furthered by investigations of such unprestigious activities as cooking. Besides, hunger is not part of the general experience of societies of this sort, especially not of the social strata to which most sociologists have belonged. At any rate, anthropologists have in the past shown more curiosity about these questions, though sociologists have now begun to follow their lead.

FOOD AMONG THE SOCIOLOGICAL CLASSICS

One looks in vain for any discussion of food and eating in the work of most of the classic sociologists. Look up 'Diet' in an index to Marx's writings, and you will find it to refer to a political assembly. To be fair, Engels recorded a fair amount of detail about the abysmal quality of working-class food in his *The Condition of the Working Class in England* (1969 [orig.1845]). But that in itself rather set the model for most later sociologists: food and food habits, when mentioned at all, were generally recorded as indicators of something else closer to the focus of sociological interest – such as social inequality – rather than as things to be explained in their own right. Of course, Marx and Engels were very conscious of food as the most basic of the means of subsistence, control over which, as Prince Kropotkin more directly signalled in his *The Conquest of Bread* (1972 [orig. 1892]), is one of the greatest themes of human history. But food as such is of only passing interest to Marx, as it is to Max Weber and Emile Durkheim. Weber casually displays his knowledge of the history of cultivated plants and domesticated animals in *The Agrarian Sociology of Ancient Civilisations* (1976 [orig. 1909]). In Durkheim's work, foods are mentioned mainly in the context of totemic interdictions and classifications of the sacred and profane in relation to lineage systems (Durkheim, 1915 [orig. 1912]: 341ff; Durkheim and Mauss 1963 [orig. 1903]: 13ff).

Among the lesser deities in the sociological pantheon the picture is only a little more promising. Herbert Spencer, like Durkheim an intellectual ancestor of both present-day sociology and anthropology, also dwelt on the religious functions of foods. He made many references to offerings of food to the dead, speculating that such oblations represented the origins of Church revenues in later stages of social development, and mentioned the part played by fasting in producing abnormal states of excitement as preparation for divining. Besides this, in dwelling on the dominance of the warrior class through much of human history (in 'militant society'), he stressed that it was based on control of food supplies. He mentioned the irritability caused by hunger when food supplies were insecure and uncertain. He also wrote interestingly about food in relation to social inequality. Sumptuary laws regulating the uses of foods, he remarked, could be traced very far back in social development, and went along with 'the subordination of the young to the old, and of females to males'. Finally, he observed that among the more curious of 'the various class-distinctions which imply superior rank by implying greater wealth', corpulence – denoting freedom from labour – was a source of pride among Chinese mandarins and admired in women in Africa (Spencer, 1888–90: I, 1, 72, 96, 157ff, 239, 205–8, 295–6).

Thorstein Veblen had a good deal to say in *The Theory of the Leisure Class* (1953 [orig. 1899]) about food and drink as means of conspicuous consumption. He drew attention to how 'the custom of festive gatherings probably originated in motives of conviviality and religion' but now 'also serve an invidious purpose' (1953: 65); how 'the consumption of choice articles of food ... becomes tabu to women and children' and members of the superior class (1953: 61). But the 'ceremonial differentiation of the dietary', Veblen contends, 'is best seen in the use of intoxicating beverages and narcotics':

> From archaic times down through all the length of the patriarchal regime it has been the office of women to prepare and administer these luxuries, and it has been the perquisite of the men of gentle birth and breeding to consume them. Drunkenness and other pathological consequences of the free use of stimulants therefore tend in their turn to become honorific ... (Veblen, 1953 [orig. 1899]: 62)

In a very characteristic essay on 'The Sociology of the Meal' (1910), Georg Simmel also begins from the ceremonial uses of food in religion from ancient times, and more generally stresses the social significance of commensality – both its prescription and proscription. Drawing his usual Kantian distinction between form and content, Simmel emphasises the consequences of the socialisation of the meal, the imposition of formal norms on the fluctuating needs of the individual making possible an 'aesthetic stylisation' of the meal independent of its actual food content, and this aesthetic stylisation then reacts back on to individual needs. Simmel illustrates the process in relation to the regularity of meals:

> We know that very primitive peoples did not eat at definite hours but anarchistically simply when someone was hungry. However, having meals together leads at once to temporal regularity, for a given circle can only gather at a previously fixed hour – the first conquest of the naturalness of eating. (1910: 245)

– as well as in some passing remarks about the development of table manners which partly anticipate the later and much more detailed work of Norbert Elias. Elias's *The Civilising Process* (1978/82 [orig. 1939]) is concerned to explain the development of manners in general among the secular upper classes in Europe since the Middle Ages, but his discussion of table manners (1978: 70–108) is particularly famous. Elias has relatively little to say about food as such although he does point to the significance of the eating of meat as a manifestation of competitive social display.

In line of succession from Simmel and Veblen, David Riesman devoted some brief but illuminating pages of *The Lonely Crowd* (1950: 142–5) to 'changes in the symbolic meaning of food' – pages which also anticipate the work of Pierre Bourdieu. Inner-directed character types of the recent American past, argued Riesman,

> ... might use food for display, with relatively standardised menus for company and for dining out; what was put on display was a choice cut of meat, an elegant table, and good solid cooking. All this was an affair largely of the women, and in many circles food was not a proper topic for dinner conversation. Having the proper food was something one owed to one's status, one's claim to respectability. (1950: 142)

In contrast the other-directed person of the mid-twentieth century in America put on display

> ... his taste and not directly his wealth, respectability, cubic capacity, or caloric soundness. ... The other-directed person is ... prepared for the search for marginal differentiation not only in what he sets before his guests but in how it is talked about with them. (1950: 142)

Herbert Blumer made passing remarks on hunger in discussing the processes through which a person constructs an act:

> First, a person has to note his own hunger. If he didn't point it out to himself, he would be merely uncomfortable and restless and would not organise himself to search for food. Then he has to define hunger in terms of whether it is something he should take care of. A glance at his watch may indicate that it is a half-hour before eating time ... Or, he may remind himself that he is on a diet ... Or he may decide he will eat. If so, he has to engage further in constructing his act. Through the use of images he points out to himself various possibilities of action – the selection of different kinds of food, different sources of food, and different ways of getting food. (1969: 95)

Blumer was right to point out how much may supervene between hunger and eating, but he makes it sound very coolly cerebral: his actor is already very self-controlled. One would hardly guess how compelling a force hunger can be. In very different mode is Pitirim A. Sorokin's *Hunger as a Factor in Human Affairs* (1975), written in 1921 as a consequence of Sorokin's direct experience in the famines which followed the Russian Revolution. With the thoroughness characteristic of his later work, Sorokin carefully classifies the forms of starvation: deficiency (or absolute) starvation and nondeficiency or comparative starvation, the latter further divided into individual-comparative and social-comparative forms, raising the problems of what was later to be called 'relative deprivation'. Sorokin then explores among other things the effects on hunger of temperament, its relation to techniques of food production, imports and exports, migration, war, criminality, riots, insurrections and revolutions, and the organisation of the state.

This brief survey of food and eating in the work of some major sociologists of the distant and the recent past is no doubt incomplete and could be extended. But it is perhaps enough to illustrate that while some notable sociologists have said enough about food and eating in passing to suggest that here is a topic potentially of considerable sociological interest, it has in the past been far from a central focus of sociology. To this day, 'food', 'eating' and 'cookery' used as keywords in searching bibliographies turn up many articles where sociologists use some food-related topic as an instance for analysing something quite other in which they are interested. For example, Suler and Bartholomew (1986), writing on 'The Ideology of Overeaters Anonymous', are predominantly interested in the ideologies and organisation of self-help groups; they could probably have as easily chosen Gamblers Anonymous or Alcoholics Anonymous. Or again, Tomlinson, in 'Thought for Food: A Study of Written Instructions' (1986), explains that he selected cookbooks rather than car repair manuals because (a) he was an 'amateur cook' (*sic* – could a woman ever so describe herself?) and had been a chef's assistant, and (b) because recipes present a relatively standard format, and thus were good for his purpose of analysing the incompleteness or indexicality of written instructions as part of the symbolic interactionists' concern with the problematics of interpretation.

Why then is the sociology of food and eating emerging as a more substantial area of research in sociology today? Such trends often have multiple causes. One influence may be the increasing awareness of nutritional problems both world-wide – mass hunger is rarely off our television screens – and within the industrial societies, where the incidence of eating disorders including anorexia nervosa, bulimia and obesity is attracting more and more attention. A second influence may be the professionalisation of nutrition and dietetics, and the increasing concern with preventative medicine, which has involved sociologists teaching health-related courses to students training in these fields. But the new interest in the sociology of food and eating also stems from some quite different sources. In particular, its upsurge seems to be connected with the rise of interest in 'the sociology of culture',[1] a popular catchall category encompassing a great deal that has been neglected as perhaps 'too trivial' by sociologists in the past. This particular rise is probably bolstered by a social respectability afforded by a shift in analytic and empirical attention from the sociologies of industrialised production to those of industrialised consumption. In turn, this has reflected a greater openness to other neighbouring disciplines, notably history and anthropology. The *Annales* school of historians has been influential in the renewal of comparative/historical sociology and the upsurge of the history of daily life. Since Fernand Braudel's celebrated call in 1961 for a history of 'material life and biological

---

[1] The Sociology of Culture section of the American Sociological Association has been one of the fastest growing sections in recent years.

behaviour', food has been among the chief interests of the *annalistes*. As for the anthropologists, food habits have always been a subject of greater theoretical interest for them than for most sociologists, and their influence on the theoretical approaches adopted by sociologists studying food and eating has been very strong.

THEORETICAL APPROACHES TO THE SOCIOLOGY OF FOOD AND EATING

Research by sociologists into food and eating has been predominantly empiricist, usually motivated by a concern with social welfare and the unequal distribution of nutrition. Early examples include investigations of the food of the poor in Britain, such as Seebohm Rowntree's *Poverty: A Study of Town Life* (1901) and Maud Pember Reeves's *Round About a Pound a Week* (1913). This concern with food and poverty has more recently been transposed on to the global level, and given new impetus through the book *Poverty and Famines* by the economist Amartya Sen (1981). Sen contends that famines are not the result of a simple shortage of food available per head of population. Even during famines, food is available; if people starve, it is because they lack the *entitlement* rights to food – entitlement through employment and earnings, through social security or through ownership. In other words, people go short of food because of the economic, social and political relationships in which they are bound up:

> ... market forces can be seen as operating *through* a system of legal relations (ownership rights, contractual obligations, legal exchanges, etc.). The law stands between food availability and food entitlement. Starvation deaths can reflect legality with a vengeance. (1981: 160)

Sen's thesis (as will be evident in Part 8 on 'Shortage and Plenty' below) has strongly influenced research by sociologists, anthropologists and historians, since it calls out for testing in famines past and present.

If for the moment we set aside research on the social distribution of nourishment as an aspect of the sociology of stratification and inequality, over the last half-century or so other theoretically-directed research by sociologists on food and eating has been too scattered for any dominant orientation to be discerned. When work by anthropologists is included too, however, it is evident that theoretical phases in this field have followed those in anthropology and sociology more widely. Broadly speaking, first functionalism, then structuralism and, more recently, developmental perspectives have been prominent. It would be going too far to speak of a succession of paradigms in the sociology of food and eating, however, because each of these fashions has been associated with research into different substantive aspects of food and eating, without any decisive invalidation of earlier approaches, questions and answers.

Functionalism

Most notable among functionalist anthropologists with a specific interest in food and eating was Bronislaw Malinowski's student Audrey Richards (1932, 1937, 1939; Richards and Widdowson, 1936). Richards set the production, preparation and consumption of food in their social and psychological context, seeking to show how, in the southern African tribes she was studying, these were related to the life-cycle, interpersonal relationships and the structure of social groups. Especially characteristic of the functional approach was a concern with how foodways expressed or symbolised a pattern of social relations. Food-seeking activities necessitated and fostered co-operation within the human group. The preparation and receiving of food played their part in the maintenance of social structures; thus 'the preparation of porridge ... is the woman's most usual way of expressing the correct kinship sentiment towards her different male relatives' (Richards, 1939: 127). This mode of reasoning is subject to all the standard objections – teleology, circularity, atemporality and so on – levelled at functionalism in sociology and anthropology generally; on the other hand, with the rise of neo-functionalism in the 1980s, sociologists are now a little more aware of its strengths as well as its weaknesses. This, however, is not the place to discuss them at length.[2]

A vaguely functionalist orientation also unconsciously underlies much collaboration between sociologists and nutritionists, a common form of

---

[2] For a fuller discussion of the functionalist approach in this area, see Goody (1982: 12–17), Fischler (1990: 15–17), and also Khare (1980). Besides Richards, Margaret Mead (1943a, 1943b, 1949, 1957, 1970) also wrote on the cultural shaping of food preferences. Given the traditional association in most societies of cooking with women's roles, it is hardly surprising that two very distinguished female anthropologists who pioneered an ethnographic focus on women should have been drawn to write on food habits.

research in recent decades, in which current nutritional science is used to evaluate the results of questionnaire or interview surveys of what people eat. When nutritionists – or nutritionally-expert sociologists – go beyond this to consider *why* people eat particular things, the resulting explanations often have a somewhat ad hoc character. For instance, Yudkin (Yudkin and McKenzie, 1964: 15–19) contended that on the whole there is a direct relationship between palatability and good nutritional value – that, for example, protein-rich animal foods are in general tastier than starch-rich vegetable foods. But he admitted that the activities of modern food manufacturers now permitted a very significant degree of dissociation between palatability and nutritional values. Besides, the correlation is plausible only if the standards of palatability which prevail in the familiar world of Europe, North America and similar countries are taken as a yardstick. In fact, not only are there very different ideas of palatability in other cultures but European-type standards are equally culturally conditioned and by no means unchanging.

Structuralism: Lévi-Strauss, Douglas, and (partly) Bourdieu and Fischler

The great virtue of the structuralist approach is that it clearly recognises that 'taste' is culturally shaped and socially controlled. It thus avoids the ad hoccery, biological reductionism and implicit ethnocentrism found in some of the work just mentioned. Its weakness, arguably, is that in avoiding any suspicion of ethnocentrism it moves so far to the pole of extreme cultural relativism that it overlooks any possibility of explaining differing food habits – particularly their origins – in terms of purpose, function or utility.

Structuralism has made itself felt in the sociology of food and eating via the influence of anthropologists like Claude Lévi-Strauss and Mary Douglas, and the semiologist Roland Barthes. In contrast to the some-what utilitarian slant of the social nutritionists and the functionalists, the structuralists have always focused more on the æsthetic aspects of food and eating: in Fischler's phrase, 'while the functionalists looked at food, the structuralists examined cuisine' (1990: 17). As Mary Douglas has argued,

> Nutritionists know that the palate is trained, that taste and smell are subject to cultural control. Yet for lack of other hypotheses, the notion persists that what makes an item of food acceptable is some quality inherent in the thing itself. Present research into

palatability tends to concentrate on individual reactions to individual items. It seeks to screen out cultural effects as so much interference. Whereas ... the cultural controls on perception are precisely what needs to be analysed. (1978: 59)

Douglas defines the aesthetic as distinct from the nutritional aspects of food as 'that part which is subject to pattern-making rules, like the rules of poetry, music or dance', adding that 'the explanation of any one such rule will only be found in its contribution to the pattern it helps to create' (1974: 84).

That remark encapsulates the structuralist approach to food and eating, the story of which begins, however, with Claude Lévi-Strauss rather than Mary Douglas. Food played a considerable part in Lévi-Strauss's work as a whole because, as Claude Fischler (1990: 17) remarks (echoing Freud's observation on dreams and the unconscious), the categories of the culinary domain constituted for Lévi-Strauss a 'royal road' in a double sense. On the one hand, they led towards an understanding of particular cultures and societies because, according to him, the cuisine of a society is a language into which that society unconsciously translates its structure, and from which its hidden contradictions can be uncovered. On the other hand, they led towards a revelation of the fundamental structures of human thought, even though the contents assigned to them are peculiar to each society (see Lévi-Strauss 1964, 1965, 1968).

Lévi-Strauss's celebrated 'culinary triangle' (1965, 1968) relating the three poles of the raw, the cooked and the rotten to human thinking about 'nature' versus 'culture', is the most famous example of his exploration of the 'royal road' in the direction of universal patterns of the human mind. It has been criticised, even ridiculed, as empty speculation (see Goody, 1982: 17–29; Mennell, 1985: 6–10; Murcott, 1988a; and, a little more sympathetically, Fischler, 1990: 43–49). Even when Lévi-Strauss looked at particular cuisines rather than seeking human universals, as in his analysis (1978 [orig. 1968]: 86) of French and English cuisines in terms of contrasting binary 'gustemes', his conclusions can be see as little more than an overly-intellectual reworking of popular stereotypes (Mennell, 1985: 7–8). (In mitigation, it can be said that this example was an amusing aside to essays on the relevance of linguistic analysis to anthropology, and that for this purpose stereotypes may be as relevant as the cuisine *an sich*.)

Structuralism since Lévi-Strauss has concerned itself more with variability and much less with universality, 'no doubt retreating from the notion of "human nature" which was suspect in its eyes', and it was 'thus that cultural relativism gained its ascendancy in the study of human eating' (Fischler, 1990:17). Lévi-Strauss's structuralism has had less direct influence on the sociology of food and eating than that of Mary Douglas. Unlike him, Douglas does not expect to find any universal message, valid for all humankind, encoded in the language of food. Yet at the same time, since research into small remote societies 'suggests that each individual, by cultural training, enters a sensory world that is presegmented and prejudged for him', she shares Lévi-Strauss's general hope that research into the cultural aspects of food habits will eventually enable us at least 'to discover the principles and ranking of tastes and smells' (1978: 59) – but the actual segmentation and ranking will differ from one society to another. Douglas's article 'Deciphering a Meal' (1972) has been particularly influential. What Douglas sought to decipher was in fact not a meal, but whole sequences of meals. Analysing the food system of her own household, Douglas writes:

> Between breakfast and last nightcap, the food of the day comes in an ordered pattern. Between Monday and Sunday, the food of the week is patterned again. Then there is the sequence of holidays and fast days throughout the year, to say nothing of life cycle feasts, birthdays and weddings. (1972: 62)

There is a very clear idea of what should constitute Christmas dinner; Sunday dinner provides a lesser peak during each week; and meals are ordered in a scale of importance in relation to each other, by the addition or omission of an item, through the week and the day down to the meanest pause for a snack. Fieldwork among a number of London working-class families by one of Douglas's graduate students revealed tea and biscuits as the lowest link in the food system (Douglas and Nicod, 1974). For the chain which links meals together gives each its meaning. Food categories encode social events, as Douglas puts it – they express hierarchy, inclusion and exclusion, boundaries and transactions across boundaries. Thus, in the Douglas household, drinks were shared with strangers, acquaintances and workmen, but meals were shared only with family, close friends and honoured guests; so the meal structure serves to maintain external boundaries, and significant social thresholds are crossed when a guest is invited to share a meal. The food system also discriminates occasions simply within the family. Douglas ascribes to its unconscious power her family's discontent at the proposal that supper be cut down for once to a single substantial dish of soup. More courses were necessary, because otherwise it wouldn't be supper.

Since her early essays, Douglas has drawn evidence for such food systems from many different cultures, and has attempted to measure quantitatively the intricacy of such rule systems (Douglas and Gross, 1981). She has related 'the artificial necessity that dominates human eating patterns' to Durkheim's conception of the creation of forms of social necessity; Douglas and Reumaux (1988) conclude that eating habits reflect a moral and intellectual pressure to create models of perfect series.

Roland Barthes deserves mention as a structuralist influence on the sociology of food and eating, on the strength of his essay 'Pour une psycho-sociologie de l'alimentation contemporaine' (1961) and his more playful short essays on food in *Mythologies* (1957). Barthes, too, sought the code or grammar underlying people's preferences in the foods they eat. His particular focus was on the semiotics of food advertising and cookery writing. From America, Barthes takes the example of the contrast between bitter and sweet flavours (in chocolate, for instance) which tends to be associated with a contrast between upper and lower classes, and also points to the interesting opposition Americans often draw between sweet and crisp foods – not logical, but often significant. In France, he pointed to sexuality, health and the sense of the past in advertising. However – and here Barthes' thinking is characteristic of structuralism in general – it was a matter of the *sense* of the past rather than the past itself as a real influence. The past, considered as an objective record, did not constitute the contemporary food system so much as to serve as a place where potent meanings could be quarried in a more or less arbitrary way. For example, Barthes insightfully sketches the contemporary connotations and social functions of a certain kind of chic 'ornamental cookery' (1957: 128–30) then to be found in the recipe columns of *Elle*, but fails to notice that this style was derived from one created in quite different circumstances and for a different social class in the mid-nineteenth century, which was by the 1950s completing its trickle down the social hierarchy before becoming extinct (Mennell, 1985: 250–5).

Attention to the past in the shaping of the present is one quality which makes Pierre Bourdieu an interstitial figure between the structuralist theorists and the later 'developmentalists' whom we shall discuss shortly. Bourdieu can be enlisted as a sociologist of food and eating largely on the basis of his book *La Distinction* (1979), subtitled *A Social Critique of the Judgement of Taste*. It deals not just with people's choices of food but with several other aspects of behaviour (clothes, furniture, music, visual arts, cinema, literature) which are often attributed to individual 'taste'. People make individual choices, apparently according to their own preferences, and yet at the same time what these preferences will be is highly predictable if we know a person's social background. The link with social stratification is close, and lower-class individuals are said to have 'vulgar' tastes and upper-class ones 'refined' tastes. The struggle over 'titles of cultural nobility' has gone on for centuries, says Bourdieu, and in this respect his explanation for the social genesis of tastes, emphasising the competitive struggle between groups in society for marks of social 'distinction', is more historically informed than the approaches of Lévi-Strauss, Barthes and Douglas.

Yet although Bourdieu would not describe himself as a structuralist, he has perhaps been locked in a community of arguments with structuralists, and with so-called 'structuralist Marxists', for so long that his own writings have taken on a certain flavour of theirs. Bourdieu explains (in the Preface to the English-language edition of his book) that his study arose out of an endeavour to rethink Max Weber's concepts of class (members of which share a common position in relation to the means of *production*) and *Stand* (members of which share a common lifestyle or position in relation to *consumption*). However, Bourdieu's preoccupation with the *reproduction* of culture from generation to generation makes his theory appear rather undynamic and, at first glance, gives it a surprisingly close resemblance to the writings of Louis Althusser and the structural Marxists. The curiously static quality is introduced into Bourdieu's theory by arguing that each individual is assigned from the beginning to a class position, defined by the amount of economic and symbolic (meaning mainly educational) capital of which it disposes. Only to a very limited extent, he argues, can this inheritance be modified by strategies of social mobility. Now, just as Lévi-Strauss and Barthes looked for a fixed code or grammar underlying the food preferences of different societies, so Bourdieu looks for formulae underlying the cultural preferences of each class or subclass:

> ... the spaces defined by preferences in food, clothing or cosmetics are organised according to the same fundamental structure, that of the social space determined by volume and composition of capital. Fully to construct the space of life-styles within which cultural practices are defined, one would first have to establish, for each class and class fraction, that is, for each of the configurations of capital, the *generative formula* of the habitus which retranslates the necessities and facilities characteristic of that class of (relatively) homogeneous conditions of existence into a particular life-style. (1979: 230 [p. 208 in English edition] – our italics)

The work of Claude Fischler – who along with Christiane Grignon and Claude Grignon is the most prolific of French sociologists of food and eating – shows the principal influence of structuralism, and yet at the same time Fischler also shares in the criticisms levelled at that tradition. Like Goody (1982: 29), he finds the attempt to define biological factors out of the explanation of social patterns the least satisfactory part of the legacy of Durkheim (Fischler, 1990: 12ff), and for him 'nature/culture' is a 'false dilemma' (1990: 48–59; 1980). As a sociologist deeply immersed in empirical data on French eating habits over the last two decades, Fischler is highly conscious of change and the necessity of explaining it sociologically. (In this respect, like Mennell, Fischler [1990: 17–19] is somewhat critical of Bourdieu.)

In long-term perspective, Fischler speaks of a contrast between the *mangeur éternel* and the *mangeur moderne*; the species *Homo sapiens* is 'an omnivore whose biological characteristics, forged through evolution by shortage and uncertainty, a few decades of abundance have not yet been able to modify' (1990: 11). Fischler has spoken (1988: 277–9) of 'the omnivore's paradox' and the resulting 'omnivore's anxiety'. The paradox is that, on the one hand the biologically-rooted human character of omnivorousness implies autonomy, freedom, and adaptability: 'Unlike specialised eaters, an omnivore has the invaluable ability to thrive on a multitude of different foodstuffs and diets, and so to adapt to changes in its environment' (1988: 277). On the other hand, unlike specialised eaters, an omnivore cannot obtain all the nutrients it needs from one food: it has an absolute need of some minimum variety. Thus:

> On the one hand, needing variety, the omnivore is inclined towards diversification, innovation, exploration and change, which can be vital to its survival; but, on the other hand, it has to be careful, mistrustful, 'conservative' in its eating: any new, unknown food is a potential danger. (1988: 278)

And hence 'the omnivore's anxiety'. That anxiety or ambivalence between 'neophilia' and 'neophobia', is of course a powerful force behind the development of the many diverse systems of culinary rules developed in human cultures, the systems of rules on which structuralists have focused attention.

In shorter-term perspective, however, rapid changes in eating habits have produced what Fischler in a much-cited essay (1979; see also 1980) called 'gastro-anomie'. The very codes or structures governing eating habits that the structuralists pursued have, since the 1960s particularly, been undergoing a process of 'destructuration' (1990: 203–7). Fischler's book *L'Homnivore* (1990) represents both a summation of his own extensive writings and an end-point to the structuralist dominance over the sociology of food and eating in France, for it shows a marked convergence with the more developmental perspectives emerging in Anglo-Saxon sociology during the 1980s.

Developmentalism: Harris (partly), Goody, Mennell and Mintz

Anne Murcott (1988a) has grouped together the books of Harris (1986), Goody (1982), Mennell (1985) and Mintz (1985) as representing a 'materialist' response to structuralism. Although that would be Harris's own preferred self-description, at least one of the other three (the one who happens to be a co-author of the present report) would object to the designation. We would now prefer (harmony is achieved amongst the present authors) to describe them collectively as, to varying extents, 'developmentalist'. They share a dissatisfaction with the structuralist legacy, but there is considerable common ground between the structuralists and the developmentalists. The latter do not at all deny the power of the symbolic meanings of food in shaping and controlling social behaviour. Nor would they fail to acknowledge that, even if he dressed it in metaphysical garb, Lévi-Strauss was making an important connection when he related the activity of cooking to 'nature' and 'culture'.

This connection has been set in developmental context by Goudsblom (1992, Chapter 3; cf. Perlès, 1979), drawing on recent discussions of the origins of the human species. Probably the first cooked foods consumed by hominids were seeds and meat accidentally roasted and found in naturally-occurring wildfires. But it would be a 'short step' (Brewer, 1978) from there for hominids to gather seeds or hunt small animals and cook them in these natural ovens. And subsequently, at least by the time of *Homo erectus*, the active use of fire for cooking was mastered. From these earliest origins onwards, however, 'nature' and 'culture' stood not in static contrast but in dynamic interaction with each other. Cooking opened up new food resources, broadening the range of edible vegetable matter in particular available for human consumption. On the other hand, the regular consumption of a wide range of cooked food most probably influenced the biology of the human digestive system in the long run (Stahl, 1984) so that cannot be assumed to be a 'natural' constant. Besides having these nutritional effects, cooking, also – Goudsblom argues – affected social organisation and mentality.

What may be said about control of fire in general applies even more to cooking: it became exclusively *and* universally a human skill, requiring not only certain biogenetic preconditions, but social organisation and cultural transmission as well. The 'short-step' noted by Stella Brewer eventually became a seven-league stride as cooking developed into a complex set of activities which was far removed from the simple reflex chain of hunger, food-seeking, eating .... The higher productivity yielded by cooking could be attained through the same forms of co-operation and division of labour which had enabled groups to control fire .... Like the control of fire, cooking is an element of culture. It has to be learned, and such learning is done in groups. It demands some division of labour and mutual co-operation and, in the individual, attention and patience. One has to watch the food from time to time and to postpone eating it until it is well cooked and has cooled off a little. (Goudsblom, 1992: 34–5)

Thus, cooking may well have played a significant part in the development of human mental capacities and social dispositions – though the developmental perspective puts this in a very different light from Lévi-Strauss's more one-sided mentalistic approach.

Marvin Harris's *Good to Eat: Riddles of Food and Culture* (1986) is determinedly anti-structuralist. The very title is an allusion to Lévi-Strauss's famous dictum that some foods are 'good to think'. Harris contends that 'whether they are good or bad to think depends on whether they are good or bad to eat' (1986: 15). It has long been known that no human group eats everything of potential nutritional value available to it. They all have patterns of preference and aversion, but how are these to be explained? The geographer Simoons (1961) surveyed the food avoidances of the Old World and showed that none of the commonsense explanations – such as that people do not eat animals they domesticate as pets – holds water. Anthropological orthodoxy is that the connection between food objects and their meanings is arbitrary, and therefore no instrumentalist explanation of food avoidances can be valid. This is the view that Harris sets out to challenge. He sets out to calculate the practical costs and benefits which, in broad ecological context, underlie some of the most perplexing food preferences and avoidances, though he admits this is no easy matter.

Each puzzling food item has to be seen as part of a whole system of food production, a distinction must be made between long- and short-term consequences, and one must not forget that food is often a source of wealth and power for the few as well as of nourishment for the many. (1986: 17)

One of the puzzles tackled by Harris is that of the sacred cow in India. While not doubting its symbolic power, Harris questions how the ban on slaughter arose. He points out that in the Rig Veda, the sacred texts of early Hinduism, the slaughter and sacrifice of cattle were central activities. Harris argues that with rapidly rising population – itself made possible by the spread of agriculture using the ox-drawn plough – this could no longer be sustained. Beef-eating became increasingly the privilege of the Brahman priestly and Kshatriya warrior castes, while peasants and tradespeople increasingly ate grain, legumes and dairy products. Long before modern nutritional knowledge, people must have been aware of the inefficiency of meat-production compared with grain production as a means of generating nourishment for humans: if grain is consumed by cattle, nine out of ten of the calories in the grain and four out of five grams of protein are lost for human consumption. In the face of this, there arose popular religious movements like Buddhism and Jainism totally opposed to killing. In the ensuing conflict of religions, Hinduism eventually triumphed – Buddhism disappeared from the subcontinent by the eighth century AD – but not before the Buddhist and Jain opposition to meat-eating had been adopted by the high castes. The nutritionally more efficient use of dairy produce survived in all castes, as did the essential use of the ox by the peasant.

Harris's explanation is thus implicitly developmental, even in a sense evolutionary. Solutions that 'fit' a particular ecological context are hit upon, usually less by rational deliberation than through unplanned social conflict. The mechanisms generating a range of possible solutions may be in part random (though processes of social development often resemble Lamarckian more than purely Darwinian evolution), but the mechanism through which one solution emerges is not random, involving as it does selection for an ecological context. Ecological context, however, must be understood to include the prevailing social as well as physical circumstances. Once outcomes are established, they are perpetuated by powerful symbolism and internalised repugnances. The symbolism may seem arbitrary now, but was not so in its origins.

Harris tackles a number of other cases, such as the Jewish and Islamic taboo on pork, the eating and non-eating of horse flesh, dogs and other pets, and milk avoidance (for example in China). It is fair to say that his views are controversial among anthropologists.

Goody (1982) and Mennell (1985) are both less concerned with the traditional anthropological question of preference for and avoidance of particular foods than with the development of systems of cuisine as a whole. The substantive content of these books is mainly discussed in the section on 'The Development of Culinary Cultures' below (Part 2). What is *theoretically* distinctive about Mennell's book, however, is that it is explicitly an application to the study of 'culinary culture' of Norbert Elias's 'process sociology' (Mennell, 1989) and particularly of the theory developed in Elias's books *The Civilising Process* (1978/1982 [orig. 1939] and *The Court Society* (1983 [orig. 1969]). Elias traced changes in personality make-up and forms of cultural expression in Europe since the Middle Ages, relating them to broader processes of change in the structure of society, particularly the internal pacification of territory in the course of state-formation. Mennell takes over from Elias an understanding of how broad social, political and economic changes shape the expression of emotion, manners, taste and lifestyle, and he applies this in accounting for changing food preferences and emerging cuisines.

In highly simplified form, Mennell's argument is that taste in eating, even appetite itself (see Mennell, 1986a, 1987a) is formed in the same way that Elias details the shaping of personality make-up more generally. The transition from the medieval oscillation between feasting and fasting, plenty and want, to an emphasis on discrimination at table parallels – indeed is an aspect of – the broader shift in the balance between external constraints and self-constraints. In early modern Europe, food supplies improved; but, more than that, the extension of trade, the progressive division of labour and the process of state formation and internal pacification improved the *security* of food supplies.

Continued improvement meant that wider sections of society were in a position to emulate an elite that hitherto had been distinguished by, inter alia, their 'gargantuan appetite'. Once food supplies were more plentiful and reliable, the aristocratic 'blow-out' stopped: this means of asserting distance between themselves and upstarts immediately beneath them in the social hierarchy reached its physical limit. Groaning boards became vulgar, ever more elaborate but delicate concoctions the height of good taste. More internalised self control became valued more than the brute capacity to stuff. This was in turn eventually reflected in social disapproval of obesity (again gradually moving down the social scale); and, for females especially, the social pressure towards self-restraint and ever thinner body-images has been associated with a rising incidence of eating disorders like anorexia nervosa and bulimia (Mennell and Simons, 1989). This theoretical perspective thus gives historical context to the very extensive body of research on eating disorders (see Chapter 6).

Underlying Sidney Mintz's *Sweetness and Power* (1985), a study of the supply of and demand for sugar, is yet another theoretical orientation, that of world-systems theory; but the outcome has much in common with Harris, Goody and Mennell. Mintz, too, is critical of structuralism, arguing that meaning is not simply to be 'read' or 'deciphered', but arises from cultural applications. Meaning is the consequence of activity, and 'not to ask how meaning is put into behaviour ... is to ignore history again' (1985: 14). He traces the development of European sugar-cane plantations in the West Indies and elsewhere from the early sixteenth century – involving indentured labour slaves, and the rise of factory-like time discipline in the colonies possibly before it arose in the home economies – and the creation of a mass market for sugar especially in Britain, the Netherlands and the USA. 'Sugar surrendered its place as a luxury and rarity and became the first mass-produced exotic necessity of a proletarian working-class'. The consumption of sugar per capita in Britain increased 25 times between 1700 and 1809, and five times more in the nineteenth century. For all the evidence of humans' innate liking for sweetness, Mintz demonstrates beyond reasonable doubt that this huge increase can only be explained in terms of the interaction through time of economic interests, political power, nutritional needs and cultural meanings. Interestingly in view of the prominence of social competition and emulation in the work of Mennell and Goody, Mintz argues that the adoption of sugar and sweet manufactured foods by the working class in the nineteenth century had little to do with imitation, but arose in a different context, from the pursuit of calories, not of display.

SUMMARY

This introductory section has surveyed the broad theoretical orientations that sociologists and other social scientists have brought to bear on the study of food and eating in human society; and, in so doing, we hope we have helped to demonstrate the significance and interest of food and eating for the discipline more widely. These theoretical issues will also serve as an orientating map for the report as a whole, though we do not pretend that they all arise equally in every one of the more specialised sections which follow.

The next three sections, dealing with the development of culinary cultures, ethnological food research, and nutritional trends, are grouped together because they all contain broad and general reviews of sociological, anthropological, historical and socio-biological areas of research. The section on nutritional trends then leads on to three sections dealing with health-related topics: food and health, eating disorders, and patterns of food consumption in relation to class, sex and age. There follow three further sections dealing with broad processes on a global level: shortage and plenty, food technology, and the impact of colonialism, migration and ethnicity on eating habits. Finally comes a group of sections which deal with cooking and eating in relation to various kinds of social institutions: professional cookery in its many forms, cooking in the context of the domestic sphere, and in 'total institutions'. We are aware that many other rationales could have been equally plausible. There are many examples of authors being mentioned in several different sections; we have sought to remove sheer repetition, but balanced that against retaining the kind of overlap which has the advantages of making sections intelligible independently of each other, and also of drawing the reader's attention to connections between issues covered in different sections.

The Development of Culinary Cultures

'Culinary culture' is a shorthand term for the ensemble of attitudes and tastes people bring to cooking and eating. Since 'culture' is understood in sociology and anthropology to mean all that is 'learned, shared and transmitted' among groups of human beings from generation to generation, it is not surprising that the idea of culinary culture has been associated with research of an historical-sociological kind aimed at explaining how different social groups – especially different societies or nation-states – came to *develop* different tastes and attitudes over time.

Jack Goody, in *Cooking, Cuisine and Class* (1982), asks why a 'high' (elite) and correspondingly 'low' (peasant) cuisine emerge in some societies but not others. It cannot, he argues, be merely a matter of degrees of social and political complexity. For no high cuisine developed in most African 'traditional' societies, yet some of those societies are notable for their greatly differentiated social and political structures.

He begins with a comparison of two North Ghanaian tribes among whom he has conducted fieldwork, the Lo Dagaa and the Gonja. There are marked differences between the two, the former having no tradition of chiefship, the latter a long history as an independent kingdom composed of a ruling estate and commoners as well as slaves. The physical environment and associated agriculture are different. Rules of ceremony, hospitality and exchange are also different, the Gonja marking festival occasions by preparing and distributing food that is cooked, whereas at Lo Dagaa festivals it is distributed raw. For the Lo Dagaa, the basic diet – with little day-to-day variation – is a porridge of guinea-corn, or millet, accompanied by a soup made mostly from ground-nuts or one or other type of leaf. Among the Gonja, yams form the basis for part of the year, and grains and cassava for the remainder, with more evidence of fish and wild meat as a relish.

And yet, despite such considerable differences of social structure in general, and in foodstuffs in particular,

... the actual shape of the cuisine in both societies was surprisingly similar. We did not discover any major differentiation of cooking either on a periodic basis, for festivals, or in relation to the different strata of Gonja society. (Goody, 1982: 96)

At this point, Goody turns to those societies for which differentiation of cuisine is a hallmark. He considers Ancient Egypt and India, ten centuries of China and of western Europe right through to the development of industrialised eating in Europe and trends towards a world cuisine. He finally comes full circle, noting the impact of the world system in the demand for, among other things, tinned sardines, tomato paste and bottled beer in the West Africa where his study began.

This broad comparative evidence leads Goody to look more closely at the types of social and political differentiation within societies. It is not enough to say that the Gonja are 'more differentiated' that the Lo Dogaa, and expect the degree of differentiation of cuisines to be commensurate. Some of the African societies may be differentiated, but the differences are not very extreme: there are still some close links between the different strata, and sub-cultural differences are not great.[3] Stratification systems with these characteristics Goody calls 'hieratic' (somewhat oddly, because it has nothing to do with priests), as opposed to the 'hierarchical' stratification systems represented by Indian castes, Medieval feudal estates or the class structures of modern industrial societies.

Drawing on his earlier work on literacy (1968, 1977), Goody also argues that this can play a part in the differentiation of the high and the low both in social structures and cuisines. His point is not just that literacy is more closely associated with hierarchical societies whereas oral tradition used to dominate 'hieratic' societies, but that literacy can have multiple social consequences. It can be, as Goody puts it, an instrument of enlightenment – for instance it offers the potential for the complex elaboration of repertoires, including the culinary, and it can be a means by which those aspiring to higher status can teach themselves the menus and manners of elite groups. But he also points out that literacy can be an instrument of oppression: until the advent of modern mass literacy, societies with writing were stratified by their access to the written word, and such restricted literacy serves to sharpen

----

[3] 'Difference' and 'differentiation' are of course relative terms requiring careful definition. An interesting comparison with Goody's two West African tribes is provided by Igor de Garine's study of the Massa and Mussey of Cameroon and Chad (1980), which relates subtle differences in social organisation and environment between superficially very similar societies to equally subtle differences in food habits.

differences in life-style and taste in all manners of things – including, of course, cuisine.[4]

A third element in Goody's explanation of the emergence or non-emergence of *hautes cuisines* relates to the organisation of households and structures of kinship. Here the sexual division of labour is especially significant. In most African societies, even for people of high rank, kitchen work is done by wives, who provide the homely dishes of domestic cuisine common to most households throughout the society. By contrast, food preparation for the elites and aristocracies of hierarchical societies has generally been the business of servants and male professionals. Goody notes that from Ancient Egypt onwards, the emergence of courts and courtiers in the midst of warrior societies has always been associated with males taking over from females in the elite kitchen.

Courtly society and the differentiation between a (mainly female dominated) domestic cuisine and a (mainly male dominated) professional *haute cuisine* is also one of many themes running through Stephen Mennell's *All Manners of Food* (1985). Mennell's central question is why an elite or *haute cuisine* developed in France but not in England. He differs from Goody in arguing that in order to understand the subtleties of differences in taste on either side of the English Channel, it is not enough to look just for differences in the degree of social differentiation. One has to compare the social development of the two nations in some detail. In fact, set against the great variety of societies examined by Goody, England and France are very similar. The differences which have developed between English and French cookery and culinary tastes, argues Mennell, are more subtle and difficult to pin down than the reciprocal stereotypes imply. Moreover, French and English cookery are *not* entirely separate things. They have been in mutual contact and influenced each other over a very long period. Since they are not wholly independent, the differences and similarities between them can only be understood in developmental perspective.

In the Middle Ages, Mennell contends, though there were striking differences in what and how the estates of society ate, there were broad similarities in how each of the estates ate across most of western Europe. The gradual emergence of recognisably 'national' cuisines broadly paralleled the formation of nation-states. But there were marked

---

[4] For a further discussion of the complex impact of the printed cookery book in western Europe, see Mennell (1985: 64–69).

differences between England and France, related to differences in the processes and outcomes of competition within complex patterns of social stratification. The French tradition of *haute cuisine* essentially took shape in court society under the absolutist monarchy in the last century and a half of the *ancien régime*. More than in England, aristocratic life in France centred on the royal court, a hotbed of intrigue and competition; the nobility became more and more like the king's personal servants, less and less engaged in governmental power, so that elaborate social display and virtuoso consumption became their essential means of self-expression. This was much less true of the nobility and gentry of England, where the Civil Wars had decisively shifted the balance between monarchy and aristocracy and where the latter still possessed considerable political power and regional bases. These differences were reflected in the French preference for elaborately prepared sauces and made dishes – costly in time, labour and ingredients – in contrast to the more simply dressed meats and puddings of their English counterparts. Not only did the newer French 'cuisine of impregnation' mark a more decisive break with the older 'cuisine of mixtures', but the dominant model of cookery in England remained that of the *country* gentry living off the seasonal produce of its land. French courtly food, in contrast, depended for its complexity on the availability of manifold ingredients in urban markets, and was thus essentially urban in character. Even though England was, by the eighteenth century, more highly urbanised than France, the *prestige* of the country life remained much higher in England.

When he reaches the nineteenth century, Mennell's argument takes on a flavour of cultural dependency theory. After the Revolution, French *haute cuisine* underwent rapid development in the hands of restaurant chefs competing with each other for the patronage of a wider gourmandising public. It was then that England – and many other European countries, and the USA besides – experienced French culinary colonisation, as upper classes adopted French chefs and French dishes. English cookery suffered a coarsening as the social elite abandoned older English traditions of eating, and perhaps also as very rapid urbanisation and population growth disrupted the transmission of those traditions.

British and French culinary cultures have been particularly well served by social historians. Besides Mennell's book, for England should be mentioned Drummond and Wilbraham's classic *The Englishman's Food* (1939), the three editions of Burnett's *Plenty and Want* (1966; 1979; 1989) and, for the post-war period, Driver's *The British at Table*,

1940–80 (1983). For France, there are many studies published in the *Annales E-S-C* or in books by *annalistes* (Hémardinquer, 1970; Braudel, 1979; Forster and Ranum, 1979), including the most outstanding study of food and eating in the Medieval period by Stouff (1970). There are also Kaplan's study (1984) of the provisioning of Paris under the *ancien régime* of French cookery up to the Revolution, Jean-Paul Aron's studies (1967, 1973) of manners, menus and culinary taste in the nineteenth century, and Jean-Robert Pitte's (1991) survey of the whole range of French gastronomy. Pitte, like many other gastronomic writers, takes a disapproving view of trends in French eating since the Second World War. It is therefore valuable to have a more detached and factual account of recent trends from sociologists. Grignon and Grignon (1981, 1986b; Grignon, 1985, 1986, 1989) use secondary analysis of statistical data, questionnaire surveys and interview material to distinguish several alternative working-class food patterns, and show how they are related to different sub-groups and subcultures. Like Bourdieu (1979), they emphasise the strong element of persistence of cultural tradition and its connection with social class, as a counterweight to the view that popular life-styles lack autonomy and amount to little more than clumsy and delayed imitations of a dominant elite life-style. Pascale Pynson (1989), on the other hand, documents the rapidity of change in French culinary culture over the quarter-century 1960–86 under the contradictory impacts of fast food, culinary multiculturalism, *nouvelle cuisine*, medical opinion and the tyranny of the dietary *régime*, and the parallel growth of the food industry and distrust of its products. It is, of course, all too easy to make a discussion of persistence versus change resemble an argument about whether a glass of water is half full or half empty: precise measurement requires good historical data.

The culinary histories of other European countries appear to have been less frequently studied, but some of the trends found in France or England or both have also been observed elsewhere in Europe. Van Otterloo's study (1990) of eating and appetite in the Netherlands since 1840 shows how sheer quantitative inequalities between social strata persisted strongly until the turn of the century, since when qualitative differences have gradually become more salient. Indeed, at the present day in the Netherlands (as in many similar countries), the working class, far from lacking sufficient nutrition, is less successful than the middle class in restraining the problem of overweight, among women especially but also among men and children. Dutch domestic cookery, reflecting the social dominance of a class of prosperous merchants rather than a courtly nobility in the Netherlands, shows an emphasis on thrift and simplicity more reminiscent of England than of France or Belgium (on which, see also Mennell, 1987b). Van Otterloo notes particularly the activities of middle-class cookery teachers from the late nineteenth to the mid-twentieth centuries in reforming the cookery both of their own class and, especially, working-class housewives. This movement was part of a more general attempt at 'organised virtue' or 'civilising offensives' conducted *de haut en bas*. (Similar, if less effective and widespread, campaigns were seen in many other countries during this period.) Van Otterloo traces the mechanisation and 'chemicalisation' of the Dutch food industry; the growing interdependence between it and the domestic cook; the simultaneous rise of health food movements of an elite character around 1900 but gaining more widespread popularity in the 1970s, many of them vegetarian and all embodying suspicion of the industry and its products; and the effect of immigration and the advent of 'world cuisine' (see Chapter 10).

The historic political fragmentation of the German-speaking lands makes it difficult, as Barlösius (1988) demonstrates, to speak of any single German national culinary culture. Quite apart from Austria and Switzerland where French influences penetrated more deeply, in Germany proper the best-known dishes are regional rather than national specialities. From the seventeenth century, the numerous noble courts of Germany were francophone and francophile, and thus open to the influence of French chefs and their cookery. But they were model-setting centres for the wider society to a much lesser degree than in France, and middle-class domestic cookery developed in Germany in a manner more reminiscent of England with its emphasis on simplicity and thrift, though without suffering the coarsening witnessed there in the late nineteenth and early twentieth centuries. Thomas Kutsch (1990) has stressed the continuing importance of regional culinary preferences in the formation of social identies in contemporary Germany.

The European origins of the United States, as Harvey Levenstein (1988) shows, were evident as much in its culinary culture as in its political institutions. The British-American culinary heritage remained remarkably little changed until well into the nineteenth century. 'British-American culinary conservatism', observes Levenstein (1988: 4), 'can hardly be ascribed to the universally high regard with which British cuisine has been held, even by the British'. Despite greater consumption in America of, for example, corn, pork and molasses, the only marked non-British early influence on American cuisine was German. Later in the nineteenth century, however, the USA saw the same French culinary colonisation of the social heights, as well as the strong influence further down the social scale of the food of such migrants as the Italians. Levenstein stresses particularly the campaigns of middle-class food reformers from the late nineteenth century, who combined in their propaganda the findings of the rising nutritional science with an essentially nativist disapproval of migrants' cuisines. These campaigns strongly resemble the 'civilising offensives' Van Otterloo described in the Netherlands.

The dubious English heritage also features in Michael Symons' (1982) account of Australian culinary culture. Symons argues that Australia is unique as the only country that has never been an agrarian society: the continent supported hunter-gatherers, and then it supported industrial society, with really nothing in between. Apart from in the earliest years after the arrival of the First Fleet in 1788, food was never short in Australia, and 'the ease of Australian eating led to arguably the world's worst cuisine, which is nevertheless not without fascination, as a case study of purely industrial eating' (Symons, 1983: 34). Though meat was super-abundant, Australia remained extensively dependent on imported, largely industrially produced food until the mid-nineteenth century, when its own food industry began to develop. Symons identifies three periods in which industry took over the garden, the pantry and finally the kitchen, relating these to three periods of gastronomic sensibility. Central to Symons's interpretation is the view that great cuisines have developed only where there has been a long-established peasantry strongly bonded to the land. In this respect he is at odds with Goody and Mennell, who attribute the emergence of *grandes cuisines* more to highly developed social elites and social competition – something else, besides a peasantry, which Australia has lacked.

Among non-Western cuisines, the Chinese has been most studied (Anderson, 1988; Chang, 1977) – not surprising in view of its long-established image as the principal rival to French among the world's historic *hautes cuisines*. Anderson stresses the nutritional efficiency both of Chinese agriculture and cooking methods. He shows how, as in France, even the peasants wanted special dishes for special occasions: ritual and ceremony institutionalised social codes concerning honour and status, and from an early date nutrition played an important part in Chinese medical science. Nevertheless, *haute cuisine* was developed among the elites, and it is from there – via bastardisation in the USA – that modern Chinese restaurant cuisine has arisen.

There are, of course, studies of *aspects* of culinary culture (as opposed to synoptic attempts to capture a whole sequence of development involving food eating at all levels of a society) in many other countries.

Smith and Christian's *Bread and Salt* (1984) is a social and economic history of food and drink in Russia focusing chiefly on the peasant diet. Jakobson (1988) suggests parallels between changes in culinary taste and artistic trends, illustrating his argument chiefly by reference to the cookery and architecture of Poland, Bohemia and Hungary. Loveday and Chiba (1985) deal with the semiotics of food and drink in Japan, and Cooper (1986) with the nuances of social significance of table manners in Hong Kong.

Studies of the development of culinary cultures in the sense discussed in this section appear to be an emerging trend, and an area in which much research still needs to be done. They represent in a loose sense a macrosociological current within the sociology of food and eating; in this respect they stand in contrast with the (again loosely speaking) microsociological concerns prevalent in the area of ethnological food research, to which we now turn.

This theme covers a vast field of rather diverse research of very varying sociological relevance, scope and standard. In this area, boundaries with other disciplinary approaches to the study of food are occasionally blurred, which can sometimes be an advantage. But, although the title 'ethnological food research' suggests a specific approach to the investigation of food habits, it is not always exactly clear what such a point of view actually is. Broadly speaking, ethnologists focus on traditional elements of popular culture: practices, habits and material objects, in order to study their role in society in continuity and change. The elements of folk culture in the case of food and meals relate mainly to its preparation, composition and consumption. Many of these studies, which encompass the whole time range from prehistory to the recent past, are purely descriptive and foreign to generalising sociological purposes. Historians, anthropologists, ethnologists and folklorists are all at work in this field. *Volkskunde* (ethnology) is especially well-developed in Germany, Eastern Europe and the Scandinavian countries. Frijhof (1988: 45) has recently located this field between history and anthropology.

In the 1970s several research societies were founded with the aim of stimulating and coordinating the ethnological, anthropological and historical study of food habits. Examples are: the International Committee for the Anthropology of Food and Food Habits (founded 1968), the Ethnological Food Research Group (founded 1970) and the International Commission on the Anthropology of Food (1977), sponsored by the existing international professional organisations of anthropologists and ethnologists. Several congresses have resulted in a few well-known volumes of proceedings (Arnott, 1976; Fenton and Owen, 1977; and Fenton and Kisbán, 1986). These volumes cover a selection of the most varied subjects investigated by scholars representing the disciplines just mentioned, and also the new area of nutritional anthropology (see Chapter 4 on Nutritional Trends, and Robson, 1980), an applied specialty largely developed in the US; examples are given below. During the 1970s and 1980s the topic of food gained in popularity and a process of diversification and specialisation has been under way.

This development has resulted in, among other things, a growing interest in questions of generalisation and theory (Voskuil 1988).

As already mentioned, ethnology is closely bound up with some branches of history and of anthropology. Because of this intimate connection the three fields of research will be dealt with together here. Results of these neighbouring disciplines are only mentioned as far as they are relevant to the central stream of ethnological research.

ETHNOLOGICAL CONTRIBUTIONS

Ethnology occupies itself with a painstaking description of the regional and social distribution of traditional ways of growing, cooking and eating food in the remote or more recent past. Although its main focus is directed at the countryside and the middle and lower social strata, sometimes comparisons are made with cities and upper strata. The distribution of typical customs like the use of white or dark bread, and of material objects such as cooking utensils and ovens are examples. The precise mapping of the stages in the process of diffusion of, for instance, certain techniques of food preservation and their regional differentiation, belongs at the heart of the ethnological method (Wiegelmann, 1975).

The German scholar Günter Wiegelmann has made a most distinguished contribution to the ethnology (*Volkskunde*) of food. His *Alltags- und Festspeisen: Wandel und gegenwärtige Stellung* ('Everyday and Festive Dishes: Change and Contemporary Position') (1967) was one of the first, and is still one of the foremost works in this field. In this study he tried as conscientiously as possible to estimate the changes in the German people's food and meal patterns, mainly during the eighteenth and nineteenth centuries. He concentrates on food innovations which became more widely diffused during those centuries, but which originated much earlier. How great a lapse of time was needed from the introduction of new foodstuffs or modes of preparation – of the potato for instance – from one class to another and from one region to another, and finally to the whole of Central Europe, is one of the questions he tries to answer. Until the 1740s potatoes were known over the larger part of Germany mainly as *Armenkost* (food of the poor); they took a century to conquer the bourgeois kitchen. The consumption of coffee (and the change to the use of bread as an essential element of breakfast) required about the same period of time, but moved the other way around: from the upper social layers down, reaching the bottom strata about 1800. Wiegelmann repeatedly points to the fact that from a certain point in time (in the case of coffee, around 1800) no more valid conclusions about geographical or social routes of certain foodstuffs can be drawn because they have been generally accepted. Other examples are: cold lunches at weddings or funerals, the use of margarine, new ways of preparing meat (e.g. goulash and schnitzel) and the adoption of these dishes to festive or ordinary meals (Wiegelmann, 1967: 235–44).

Another major work on food by Wiegelmann, in cooperation with the historian Hans Teuteberg, focuses on the changes in food and meal patterns in the wake of the Industrial Revolution: *Der Wandel der Nahrungsgewohnheiten unter dem Einfluß der Industrialisierung* (Teuteberg and Wiegelmann, 1972). In this study the authors stress the special contribution of ethnology and emphasise the fact that nineteenth-century changes in dishes and meal patterns must be linked to the often far more sweeping ones in the two preceding centuries. They use social and regional differences in the various German cities and rural areas as a starting point. Important turning points in the development were to be found around 1770 (when potatoes, bread and coffee or coffee substitutes began to be used on a mass scale, setting the pattern of marking the future working class diet), and around the First World War, when (like margarine) innovations that had originated since about 1850 were diffused to broad layers of the population (1972: 225–368). A sequence of stages comparable with that described in Germany by Wiegelmann can be discerned in Britain and the Netherlands (Burnett, 1989, Van Otterloo, 1990).

Since the appearance of these trend-setting ethnological studies others have followed. In Arnott (1976) a wide range of topics is dealt with, varying from ethnobotanic change (prehistoric agricultural develop- ments and the origins of maize-growing and wine-making), the foods of the Cherokee Indians, and eighteenth century foods and cooking utensils in Maine to folk beliefs in boiling blood sausage in Sweden and the baking and consumption of several types of bread in the most different parts of the world. Fenton and Owen's collection (1977) contains an even more loosely connected range of papers, from the pretzel as a preferred food in Philadelphia, via frozen TV-dinners, the staple emergency meals of modern society, to the ethnological characteristics of traditional wheat-flour foods in Bulgaria. Although the particular contributions may be interesting in themselves – those on Greek immigrant cuisine in America (Theodoratus, 1977), on the beginnings of the modern milk industry in Germany (Teuteberg, 1977) and on the development and decline of preferences and taboos in food and drink (Tolksdorf, 1977) may be mentioned – the lack of a more general systematic or thematic approach makes this type of proceedings less useful, at least from a sociological point of view.

In the 1980s, more studies have appeared on food in popular culture (James, 1981; Voskuil, 1983; Jobse-van Putten, 1989). Voskuil describes in a very interesting article the differences in the regional and social distribution of the consumption of white and dark bread in the Netherlands since the Middle Ages; Jobse-van Putten occupies herself with the regional variation in the preservation of food in the subsistence household in the same country during the first half of the twentieth century. Proceedings of recent ethnological conferences, for example, 'Innovation in Food Habits' (Dembinska, 1986) and 'Food in Change' (Fenton and Kisbán, 1986) show a tendency to try dealing with more general themes, as is evident in the papers of Kisbán (1986) and Teuteberg (1986), dealing with periodisation and the identification of turning points in the change of European diet. Examples of this general theme in several national contexts in Europe and the United States are given in the remaining part of the book. Books of this type, we can conclude, with small variations, all harp on the same theme.

A most important recent display of ethnological learning consists in the *Festschrift* for Günter Wiegelmann on his sixtieth birthday (Bringéus et al., 1988). One of the contributors, J.J. Voskuil, criticises the (unintended) suggestion made by Wiegelmann. He had argued that, in periods of economic prosperity, innovations tend to diffuse from the centre to the periphery and from upper social layers down to the bottom, more or less automatically. This is not always the case, Voskuil asserts; reality is often more complex than we want to have it. He illustrates his thesis with the example of the process of diffusion of coffee and tea in the Netherlands, based on a source of historical data, inventories of estates and bequests, that has recently been increasingly used.

HISTOIRE DES MENTALITÉS

It is clear from the above survey that the borderline between ethnology and certain types of history is not very sharp. This is especially true for the history of daily life and the *histoire des mentalités*, associated especially with the *Annales* school and Fernand Braudel, whose call for a history of *la vie matérielle* initiated a stream of studies of the history of food extending over three decades. Some of the most interesting articles from the *Annales* have been collected in volumes edited by Hémardinquer (1970) and (in English translation) by Forster and Ranum

(1979). To mention only a few of the wide range of subjects embraced by the *Annales* historians: Jean-Jacques Hémardinquer explained the role of the family pig under the *ancien régime*, Jean Leclant studied coffee and cafés in Paris in the second half of the seventeenth century, while Guy Thuillier elucidated the system of water supply in Nivernais in the nineteenth century. Forster and Ranum's collection also includes Jean-Paul Aron's description of the art of using left-overs in Paris, which is a most remarkable example of the trade in spoiled foods in the nineteenth century, this time originating not in the sheer poverty of lower class citizens but in the wish of less well-to-do gourmets to eat high cuisine dishes from first-class restaurants. Another collection of famous contributions from (or akin to) *Annales* is that edited by Forster and Forster (1975), which contains inter alia the article by Cecil Woodham-Smith on the great hunger in Ireland in the 1840s (see also her book-length treatment of the subject: Woodham-Smith, 1962).

Historical studies on food of a more or less popular character have appeared in the last few decades on the rising tide of the interest in everyday life in the past (Pullar, 1970; Tannahill, 1973). A most interesting overview of the history of food has already been given by Stephen Mennell (1986a). He suggests that historians for a long time occupied themselves with the 'supply' side of the history of food, while the 'demand' side, the history of taste, has received less attention. Another type of study consists in the elucidation of the material conditions for cooking and eating; Field's (1984) history of cooking utensils is an example of this.

ANTHROPOLOGICAL APPROACHES

Anthropological studies on this subject have appeared with some regularity since Audrey Richards' (1932) pioneering study on hunger and work in a South African Bantu tribe. In the 1960s and 1970s there was a very clear growth of studies relating to food (see also *Communications*, 1979); theoretically-orientated studies by Mary Douglas (1966, 1975) and Lévi-Strauss (1964, 1966 [orig. 1965], 1968) and the classical study of Chang (1977) on the cultural-historical significance of food in China appeared. They converged with anthropological research of a more descriptive or practical character, directed in the first place at the solution of problem of food and culture (Mead, 1964; Fitzgerald, 1976; Wilson, 1979). Farb and Armelagos (1980: 3) express this turn to theory by saying that it represents an attempt at understanding society and culture through eating; they present a great deal of data gathered by anthropologists about the symbolic meanings of the multifarious food habits of the peoples of the world. Food in anthropology is to be seen as a means of expressing group identity, of the relationship with other groups and with the gods.

In the 1980s this growth produced an explosion of major theoretically inspired studies in the anthropology of food (Goody, 1982; Mintz, 1985; Harris, 1986) and, as Anne Murcott (1988a) has observed, we are now in the phase of real theoretical debate on different ways of interpreting eating habits, cooking, and food taboos such as the abomination of the pig, the cow or insects and other 'strange' food habits (see also Mennell, 1985).

These theoretical developments in the core of the discipline of anthropology are perhaps far away from the generally rather descriptive mode of the ethnological and anthropological methods of treating traditional foodways. Typical topics in this field are the specific function and symbolic meaning of certain traditional foods and drinks in rituals, the significance of food in the system of folk medicine and in popular religion. The discipline of 'nutritional anthropology' (see Chapter 4, Nutritional Trends) is also partly akin to ethnology (Robson, 1980; Jerome et al., 1980; Engström, 1984; Fischler, 1985).

Symbolic meanings of traditional and festive foods

The variety of topics in this corner of the field is so large that it is difficult to give a balanced impression; the choice is therefore rather arbitrary. Piette (1989) considers the functional and structuralist interpretation of festivity and the structure of folk feasts in general, and thinks these occasions have to be conceived of as a form of aesthetics. The meaning of the wedding-cake in Britain and the ceremony of cutting it are open to various changing interpretations; its form and its mixture fit into a long tradition of English feasting (Charsley, 1987b). Apart from feasts and rituals around wedding-cakes, a series of other foods and food-rituals attracted the attention of anthropologists: the diet of aboriginal Eskimos, their systems of food sharing and the reflection of change in their story-knife tales (Damas, 1972; Draper, 1977; Lippe-Stokes, 1980), Chinese table manners (Cooper, 1986), the 'aperitif' and its ritual social meaning (Clarisse, 1986). Vivier (1987) illuminates the organisation and function of the traditional garden in France as a 'pantry and a medicine-chest'. The garden is conceived of as a structured space, containing plants that serve food, medicinal, aesthetic and symbolic requirements, often all at once. The author stresses the fact that the garden is a witness to the vitality of popular culture.

Religious symbolic meanings of food in various parts of the world are also widely described. Loveday and Chiba (1988) deal with food as a symbolic code in Japanese culture; Giobellina-Brumana (1988) estimates the essential role of the sacred meal in the Afro-Brazilian Candomble Cult, which offers an alternative to the official world view and establishes identity for its members. In the author's view, the sacred meal is among other things a form of food offering; it functions as a sort of therapy and as a means of classification by relating humans and divinities. Starr Sered (1988) explains the role of cooking as a sacred act among Middle-Eastern Jewish women. For elderly women in Jerusalem the sacred is fully embedded in the profane. The women see Jewish identity, tradition, law and holiness in terms of feeding others. Many of their foods embody potent Jewish symbols, and the rituals of food preparation imbue their everyday domestic work with holiness. This type of religious practice, the author states, represents a major mode of human religious experience. The fact that religion, food and health can be very close is also shown in the case of the Seventh Day Adventists (Topalov, 1987).

CONCLUSION

In this chapter, the intention has been to display something of the colourful field of ethnological food research with as broad a brush as possible. The result was the identification of a borderland between parts of two disciplines – anthropology and *histoire des mentalités*. So far it remains difficult to estimate very precisely the overall relevance of this type of research for the sociology of food and eating. It is, however, clear that a good many instances of this kind of research are remote from styles of modern sociological inquiry.

Several related themes are subsumed under the above title: the development of nutritional science (and cognate disciplines), developments in research on food consumption, and trends in nutritional policies. We try to clarify the interrelationship between food problems on the one hand and the developments in food science, food consumption research and national and international food policies on the other. Differences and similarities between countries with economies of plenty and economies of scarcity are sketched very briefly and mention is made of the most important research themes have been mentioned.

THE DEVELOPMENT OF NUTRITIONAL SCIENCE AND COGNATE DISCIPLINES

Food can be studied from the viewpoint of many disciplines. One main stream of scholarly activity is centred on the science of nutrition. This report is clearly centred in sociology and not in nutritional science, a discipline in which none of us is expert. However, a very brief résumé of some of its most obvious features is essential for this overview. The nutritional point of view originated about 1850 in Europe (France, Germany, the Netherlands); since then it has gained in importance, due in part to the rise of the modern welfare state. The origins and growth of nutritional science were stimulated by practical problems of food and health, food storage and long-distance food transport. Nineteenth-century conditions of scarcity and ill-health among the working classes in the industrialising western European countries were also of political and public health significance, thereby also serving as contributory influences to the rise of nutritional science. Doctors visiting poor people living in overcrowded city slums came to blame inadequate food for widespread infant mortality, feebleness, ill-health and susceptibility to epidemic diseases. The growth of the food industry was another factor; standards for the safety of products were developed with the passing of national laws against food adulteration. The poor quality of food was also a sizeable problem in this period (Burnett, 1989; Van Otterloo, 1990).

Today nutritional scientists in Western countries are again stressing the importance of the relationship between food and health. They are setting standards of 'good food' and advising the public to keep to a 'prudent diet' which will maintain health. In the midst of the affluence in industrial countries, health problems have been shifted from those related to undernourishment, such as rickets, to those related to overeating. International nutritionists, connected for instance with the WHO and FAO, create the impression that they are more needed here and now than ever before, and perhaps rightly so. For the USA examples are: the *Dietary Guidelines*, issued by the National Health Institute and the *Recommended Daily Allowances*, set by the National Research Council. These and other governmental organisations sponsor a 'Dietary Guidelines Advisory Committee' which regularly revises the reports issued (see, for a Dutch version: National Food and Nutrition Board, 1986). The social value attached to food, health and physical beauty has risen constantly in the second half of the twentieth century. Thus the representatives of nutritional science have become an important part of multifaceted medical power, operating on the national and international level and influencing governmental policies as much as the use of public research funds.

This eminent position has, in the last decade, resulted in an ever-expanding collection of nation-wide data on *food consumption patterns*. This type of epidemiologically related research has revealed large-scale food problems in modern societies, at least with respect to nutritional standards. *Food policies*, aiming at dissuading people from eating too much fat or too little fibre, are now taken for granted. Yet this is, in fact, only a recent development, which had to be fought for. Both of these trends, explained more fully below, would have been impossible without the knowledge accumulated by nutritional scientists. No safety rules and standards for the production of new food items to protect the general public could have been developed, and no programmes of nutritional education could ever have been initiated. People in modern industrial societies are now aware of such things as calories or joules, and of the composition of foodstuffs and nutrients.

Nutritional science comprises aspects of biology, microbiology, biochemistry and biophysiology. Its outlook is very practical, setting itself health goals in the first place; as such it can be seen as a specialised part of medical science. As in other disciplines, there is a trend towards specialisation and differentiation. Nutritionists, while setting standards of behaviour, have found that people perhaps know about their rules, yet do not put them into practice. So some of them have begun to look to the social sciences for help. This is especially the case in the developing countries where the main nutritional problem is still undernourishment. It has resulted for instance in the new applied social science, called 'nutritional anthropology', which has developed in America and, to a lesser extent, in Europe (Freedman, 1977; Wilson, 1979; Jerome et al., 1980). Other behavioural and social sciences have contributed to the formation of such new practices and disciplinary fields as psychophysiology (Shepherd, 1990), biopsychiatry, social nutrition (Krondl and Coleman, 1986), and nutritional education. The last mentioned aims unhesitatingly at behavioural change (Edwards et al., 1985). The proliferation of relatively new journals witnesses these developments: *Ecology of Food and Nutrition*, *Journal of Nutrition Education*, *The British Journal of Nutrition*, *Ernährungsforschung*, *Cahiers de nutrition et de diététique*, to mention only a few. A further trend of specialisation is connected with specific food problems or population groups. This development is reflected in periodicals like the *International Journal of Obesity*, *Eating Disorders*, and *Journal of Nutrition for the Elderly*.

One of the important topics in the international nutritional discussion is the problem of setting uniform nutritional standards for health (Douglas, 1984a). It is a point of debate how accurate these standards are for recommending and assessing adequate nutritional intake and the nutritional status of different national populations. Comparative studies (in India and Mexico for instance) focusing on the ethnonutritional concepts of policymakers are useful for understanding ways in which standards are set. Messer (1989) suggests that in some cases small is healthy.

RESEARCH ON FOOD CONSUMPTION AND EATING HABITS

In modern Western countries, at least two types of food consumption research have been developed. These are in the first place large-scale epidemiological surveys which measure as exactly as possible 'food intake', nutritional status, health characteristics and social variables of national populations (*Assessing Changing Food Consumption Patterns*, 1981; Thomas, J.E., 1982; Diehl, 1986). Smaller-scale studies on special groups of the population, with or without biomedical and nutritional data, are also important (Freedman and Grivetti, 1984; Grignon, 1987).

Frequently one or other of these special groups – in the opinion of nutritionists – run a certain health risk if they do not eat a suitable diet. This is particularly important at several periods in the life-cycle of individuals, for instance: pregnancy, birth and infancy, youth and old age. A great deal of research therefore deals with expectant mothers, children, families, young people and the elderly (see also Chapter 7). Other groups at risk are the sick (at home or in hospitals and other institutions), the poor, students, migrants and adherents of 'alternative food systems', such as some strict forms of vegetarianism, macrobiotics and other food belief systems. Mary Harris et al. (1984), for instance, describe the food intake in a multicultural community in the South-western United States with special reference to ethnic, gender and age differences. The authors conclude that nutrition programmes and curriculum development should be adapted and tailored to fit the needs of children of different cultures, sexes and ages. Other studies are for instance directed at the social and nutritional situation of mothers and children living in extended families in Jordan (Miles and Bisharat, 1990). It appears that the child's nutritional status is strongly and adversely influenced by a mother's position of low autonomy within the family.

A great many historical and sociological studies, overviews or commentaries on food consumption, preferences and eating habits are based in part on or make use of these generally quantitatively analysed data (Essemyr, 1986; Fischler, 1986a, 1989; Grignon and Grignon 1984, 1988; Kutsch, 1986). To this category also belong studies (already referred to above) on the (long-term changes in) eating habits and taste of nations such as England (Drummond and Wilbraham, 1939), France (Pynson, 1989) and Australia (Symons, 1982) – some of them classics, others of a more popular character.

Eating and Affluence

Recently the foci of food consumption research have turned to problems of eating and health connected with the conditions of living in modern industrialized and affluent societies. One very important question is that of *fatness* and its corollaries, the so-called welfare diseases, such as cardiovascular diseases and some types of cancer. The broad spectrum of 'eating disorders' like obesity, bulimia and anorexia nervosa are also examples. Although the latter are considered psychiatric problems, they most probably would not have occurred in societies without a stable and plentiful supply of food, in which standards of health and beauty have become entangled. These high social demands have caused many difficulties for those people, especially women, failing to meet them (see Chapter 6).

Another important research theme, recently rediscovered, has to do with the social inequality in food and our health. This question belongs, in part, to the larger field of poverty studies which has a long-standing tradition. The studies by Seebohm Rowntree (1901) and Maud Pember Reeves (1913) on conditions of housing and diet among the British poor at the beginning of the twentieth century are two examples. This type of research is more often undertaken in periods of declining welfare or economic depression, and other times of hazard for groups of the population with weak income positions. For instance, among some groups hunger and malnutrition are still a problem, even in the United States of today (Fitchen, 1988). This line of food consumption research overlaps with, or even can be subsumed under, the studies discussed in Chapter 8 on Shortage and Plenty.

One final example is the recent effort to make inventories of the eating habits of elderly people – a group increasing in modern societies and expected to raise many problems in the fields of care and health. The aim of Western governments is to improve elderly people's quality of life and to try to help them live independently in their own homes rather than in institutions. The physical and financial ability to take responsibility for their own meals is a central factor in reaching these overall goals.

TRENDS IN NUTRITIONAL POLICIES

During the 1980s certain national governments, in accordance with initiatives from the FAO and WHO, started to develop national *food policies*, intended to be coherent bodies of measures. There are two main goals: first, to prevent illness and to further public health by informing people about the importance of a 'prudent diet'. People are advised in numerous ways to eat more fruits, vegetables and fibre and fewer foodstuffs containing fat. Second, a food policy purports to guarantee the safety of food products, which means issuing and enforcing rules and regulations for food producing, food processing and food distributing companies. In modern Western countries complex organisations and institutions have been set up for this purpose. These organisational networks fulfil several functions, the most important of which are *public enlightenment and education, research* and *control*. Several large-scale campaigns, for instance against the consumption of too many fatty foods, have been undertaken; these are commonly accompanied by a great deal of evaluative research. It will be clear that such policies are found mainly in countries characterised by economic abundance.

A vast amount of literature has been published on food policies, their implications and results. The Norwegian Nutrition and Food Policy for instance strives for four goals: to promote healthier eating habits, to help stabilise world food supply, to increase national self-sufficiency in food production, and to strengthen the rural economy (Kelpp-Knut and Forster, 1985). The authors report that, in spite of an integrated and minutely prepared policy, only minor changes in food consumption have been achieved (see on this particular example *inter alia* Milio, 1981; and also her commentary for Finland, 1991). Numerous articles on the evaluation and outcomes of programmes for nutrition and health education are also part of this literature. Some titles speak for themselves, for instance 'Nutrition Behavior Change. Outcome of an Educational Approach' (Edwards et al., 1985), 'Health Education and Baseline Data: Issues and Strategies in Nutrition Campaigning' (Moon and Twigg, 1988), or 'Teaching Consumers about Food Purchasing and Ecology' (Fishman, 1985). The latter author states (p. 33) that consumers in the United States must be taught how to consider health (aesthetics, budget and culture) in their food choices and to take account of ecology also. The food production and consumption of the United States today has a great many ecological consequences. In another type of literature the usefulness of these programmes of food policy in food-rich countries is debated. Duhl et al. (1985) criticise the quality of the fruit and vegetables produced by the food system in California. The author argues for measures which will lead to the development of an affordable, healthy and ecologically sustainable food supply. Harper (1988) discusses 'the misguided drive to improve the American diet'. He states that recent attempts to modify dietary practices in view of the risks of heart diseases and colon cancer is based on the faulty assumption that diet affects all individuals in the same way. Increased longevity may have increased the public's fear of diseases of old age; by dieting and taking supplements people now try to ward off ills that have never been attributable to food. Public health officials should not make blanket recommendations for an entire population, the author concludes, for this can undermine the confidence in the science of nutrition. There are signs that still other approaches are being initiated from among the social sciences: for instance, Smith's (1991) insights from political science are brought to bear in his case study of 'food-scares' in Britain in the late 1980s, and Murcott (forthcoming a) offers an overview of the relation between policy and other economic and socio-cultural trends in Britain since the Second World War.

Food policies, as far as they exist, in developing countries (preindustrial or partly industrialised) are directed to the problem of under-nourishment and short-term or long-term food shortages. Famine and hunger are often caused not by failure of food production, but are rather connected with problems of inadequate distribution of food (Douglas, 1984a: 1–7). In Douglas's view, food policies often take no account of the ways in which the use of food is embedded in the socio-cultural habits of the people whose diet it is intended to change. For this reason attempts by the FAO and the WHO to change patterns of food consumption are often doomed to failure. Part of the literature on Third World food policies is also subsumed under Chapters 8 (Shortage and Plenty) and 10 (Impact of Colonialism). Super and Wright (1985), for instance, point to the most important political and social factors which are involved in Latin American food problems. Balaam and Carey (1981) compare food policies in different regions of the world.

Food policies in the less privileged parts of the globe, often initiated by the FAO and WHO, are accompanied by a great deal of research, as in the industrialised countries. The main aim, the improvement of diet, is pursued for instance by the initiation of nutrition programmes or by the introduction of new crops to raise the income position of the small farmers (Marchione, 1984). The discipline of nutritional anthropology, already mentioned above, was developed especially to serve these policies (Fitzgerald, 1976).

Beliefs and Practices about Food and Health: the Lay Perspective

Our discussion of food and health in this section is distinguished from that on nutritional trends by its concentration not on the professional concerns of the nutritional sciences but rather on the sociological study of non-professional laypeople's apprehensions of food and health. Lying on the shared boundary of social anthropology (see Chapter 3, and particularly Messer, 1984) and sociology, the scholarly attitude involved enshrines an element of cultural relativism. It seeks to avoid privileging allopathic medical thought in order to unearth the 'identifiable counterparts' to scientific medical fields of symptomatology, nosology, aetiology and epidemiology 'in the thoughts and activities of people outside the formal medical community' (Davison et al., 1991: 6). It is, then, an attitude that parallels the relation between studies in ethnomedicine and medicine by emphasising the ethnonutritional rather than the nutritional.

This scholarly perspective surfaces, as will be seen in a moment, in studies of the food beliefs and eating habits of non-Western cultures, among nations in the process of industrialising and among migrant groups resident in Westernised nations. It also informs significant aspects of the largely North American applied speciality of nutritional anthropology to which we have just referred in the previous section (Jerome et al., 1980; Pelto et al., 1989; Prättälä, 1991). This perspective, though, is underdeveloped in studies of established industrialised peoples. Elements are detectable in historical study of European food beliefs – for instance, tomatoes were thought to be injurious to health and consequently were largely avoided until the later eighteenth century in England (Wilson, 1973). Mintz (1985), among many others, notes sugar's place in the mediaeval pharmacopoeia rather than on the table. More recently, he has extended his historically informed, political economic analysis of the symbolism of sugar. In a speculative essay on its use with almonds in the form of marzipan, he proposes a symbolic connection between whiteness and curative properties that is linked to the theme of purity and health – a theme, he argues, that runs throughout the history of this delicacy (Mintz, 1991). Empirically based studies of modern Western cultures in this vein, however, remain few and far between.

A large body of the work that is available examines versions of a humoural theory which integrates food and drink with a concern for health, both in lay thought and practice and in non-allopathic medical systems of knowledge (e.g. Anderson, 1980; Bhopal, 1986; Cosminsky, 1977; Currier, 1966; Eichinger Ferro-Luzzi, 1980; Gould-Martin, 1978; Logan and Morril, 1979; Manderson, 1981, 1987; Messer, 1981; Sukkary-Stolba, 1987). Remote temporally and culturally from modern Western (medical and scientific) thought, the classic form of this theory defines good health as the achievement of a balance between four qualities, heat, cold, wetness and dryness. Correspondingly, illness represents an imbalance. Any phenomenon or state of being is classifiable in these terms: air, disease, people, infancy, pregnancy, old age, as well, of course, as food and drink. Though commonly regarded as Hippocratic, the origin of this system of thought is obscure (Anderson, 1984). Versions are widespread today in South and South East Asia, China, Africa and in rural/peasant societies of Latin America. Examples include studies of: the use of food curatively and preventatively (Koo, 1984); the way the system is potentially subject to change in Hong Kong (Chan Ho, 1985); and as a component in mothers' management of acute diarrhoea in India (Kumar et al., 1981). They are found to be specially relevant for postpartum diets, though the 'rules' may be broken, in a Malay village (Laderman, 1984), and in the special care required during pregnancy and infancy among both Hong Kong residents in London (Tan, 1982; Wheeler and Tan, 1983) and Punjabi women in central England (Homans, 1983). And they occur as culturally meaningful 'resistance' to Westernised public health advice in Peru (Wellin, 1955) as well as in Sri Lanka (Nichter, 1985) and in conflict with nutrition education programmes among Indochinese women in Los Angeles (Fishman et al., 1988).

Two common findings are noted in this literature: one is that the four-way classification is often collapsed into a simpler two-way distinction between hot and cold; the other that the systems are highly variable, if not wonderfully flexible. Anderson notes that not only are informants reported to vary from one another in their coding of foods and diseases, not only do they change their minds over time, but that some 'even change their minds in one sentence' (Anderson, 1984: 760). No matter how variable, though, what is central to such thought is the manner in which the internal logic of the theoretical system *integrates* food, drink and health. Herein lies the significant contrast with modern styles of Western thinking about the matter (though Helman's [1978] paper 'Feed a Cold and Starve a Fever' – an aptly titled study of patients' views in his own London general practice – hints at some kind of 'remnant' of popular thought of a rather earlier era).

It is not that food and drink are left out of account in modern medical thinking, but that they figure in another fashion. Crudely stated, diet and dietary regimens lost their integral, especially diagnostic and therapeutic, place in formal and popular medical knowledge and practice with the last couple of centuries' 'ascendance of science' (Pelling, 1986). Equally crudely put, food and drink have re-emerged as twentieth-century medical concerns alongside twentieth-century patterns of (degenerative) disease – as causes of cirrhosis of the liver, and 'risk factors' in coronary heart disease, and possibly some cancers, or diabetes – and later twentieth-century versions of public health philosophy that focus on disease prevention and health promotion (WHO, 1990).

It is against this backdrop that sociological studies of food and health in industrialised nations may be viewed. Although the last two decades have seen a considerable development of work on 'health beliefs' i.e. with some ethnomedical affinity, in the US (Zola, 1973; Kleinman, 1980), France (Herzlich, 1973), Scotland (Blaxter, 1979, Williams, 1983), Wales (Pill and Stott, 1982), Australia (Pilowsky and Spence, 1977), and England (Cornwell 1984; Pollock, 1988), it is striking that food and drink figure only fleetingly. It is as if a disappearance of diet from formal medical thought is reflected twice over. In Britain at least, food and eating appear culturally and cognitively separate from health and disease (Murcott, forthcoming)[5] – part of a larger picture in which the salience of any aspect of health in everyday life in any case appears to be low (Calnan and Williams, 1991). A 'medical' sociology has emerged which marginalises investigation of the ethnonutritional.

---

[5] On the other hand, it may be that there is more continuity in folk beliefs about food and health than suggested here. In the Netherlands it appears to be reflected in the systems of beliefs and practices of alternative food movements and the vigorous growth of alternative health systems. Both there and in Britain there was a whole body of writing by medical men of the eighteenth and early nineteenth centuries which may have entered into the 'cultural undercurrents' and never really gone away. For instance, Mennell (1988) has argued that certain folk beliefs about digestibility and indigestion still prevalent in Britain appear to be related not to *current* medical opinion but to be survivals of views propagated by doctors as long ago as the beginning of the nineteenth century.

Such speculation is supported by noting that some of the few studies attending to food and health tend to be expressly addressed to newly emerging public health reformulations of health and nutrition education and health promotion – and funded accordingly. Notable among these are Pill's (1983) reporting of working-class women's conceptions of the virtues of diet in avoiding illness, and the depictions by Charles and Kerr (1988) and Van Otterloo and Van Ogtrop (1989) (all discussed elsewhere in this report) of the conflicts women experience between maintaining domestic harmony and providing their children and husbands with food they believe healthful. Occasional studies of the experience and health beliefs of pregnant women (nowadays cast as patients under medical surveillance) cannot ignore modern formulations of medical advice during the ante-natal period. MacIntyre (1983) has examined the impact of pregnancy on appetite, and Murcott (1988b) reports expectant mothers' attempts at renegotiation of their sense of self in the face of 'cravings' and 'aversions' of appetite in pregnancy.

Examination of popular thought about food and health is also to be found in the somewhat separate body of sociological literature on the social movements devoted to 'alternative' or 'counter-cultural' world-views and corresponding styles of life. Even though they appear in a different social and cultural guise from the humoural, these 'alternative' belief systems evidently also enshrine integrative popular theories of food and health. Among these studies are Atkinson's (1978) imaginative Lévi-Straussian analysis of the attribution of healthful properties to a concoction of honey and cider vinegar in rural Vermont and, in the same vein, his interpretation of the social value accorded to (commercially produced) 'health foods' in Britain (Atkinson, 1980). Other studies in this area include Roth's (1976) comparative study of the natural health movement in Germany and the USA, Whit (1990) on the USA and England, investigations of the health food movement in the eastern USA by Kandel and Pelto (1980) and in the Netherlands by Van Otterloo (1990: 184–209), and examinations of modern vegetarianisms both by Twigg (1980, 1983) and by Amato and Partridge (1989). Typically such studies reveal belief systems and preferred modes of living which seek to 'recover' a purity held to be under threat by the artificiality of over-civilised modern urban life; belief systems in which the virtue of the natural is reaffirmed. All this is expressed in a number of ways: an association between health and the consumption of minimally processed foodstuffs; the avoidance of selected, or all, animal products; a repugnance for modern stock rearing techniques; a suspicion of 'artificial' food additives and of the modern use of agricultural fertilisers and pesticides; and a generalised ecological, 'green' sensitivity (see also Chapter 9, Food Technology).

Though more and more people are reported to be reducing or avoiding meat because of a moral objection to its consumption, Keil and Beardsworth (1991) observe that there is considerable variety in the ideological justifications presented – a 'menu-pluralism' as they term it. Whit (1990) makes a similar point, noting the interlinkages among people committed to alternative food systems with yoga, tai chi, holistic healing, and so on. He also suggests an interesting parallel with Protestantism: 'Whereas Protestants took responsibility for their own *spiritual* health, the new holistic health protest-ants take responsibility for their own *bodies* (and spirits)'. There are other motives too; Ilmonen (1991) proposes, for instance, that confidence in the virtues of the natural and organic serves as a buffer to the further penetration into the pattern of Nordic eating habits of international and ethnic cuisines.

'Alternative' styles of thought shade into aspects of more widespread public appreciations of food's relation to health. The British food scares in the late 1980s – eggs were widely reported to be contaminated with *salmonella enteritidis*, certain cheeses with *listeria*, and *bovine spongiform encephalopathy* was diagnosed in cattle herds – widened public distrust of modern food production techniques. Detailed socio-logical investigation of popular belief systems in the face of the British 'scares' is lacking, though Sellerberg (1991a) suggests that distrust of food is apparent across Europe. Instead, attention has tended to focus on the role of the mass media in heightening public anxiety (Beardsworth, 1990; Gofton, 1990; and for a political science view see Smith, 1991).

The scope for further sociological study of beliefs that may link food and health is considerable. An ethnonutritional stance could valuably investigate the manner in which modern dietary advice is incorporated, modified or ignored in belief systems of different segments of industri-alised populations. Such an approach could also illuminate the extent to which popular theories about food and health inform the beliefs of doctors, nurses, perhaps even dieticians.

Sociological studies of belief are also relevant to those suffering conditions that medical science recognises as inalienably involving diet. Diabetes, for instance has received limited sociological attention so far (but see Posner, 1983; Drummond and Mason, 1990). So too have the eating disorders, in particular anorexia nervosa and bulimia. Though these are the subject of mammoth literatures in psychiatry (Farmer et al., 1986) and psychology (Cooper et al., 1984) and are the subject of a somewhat separate feminist critique (Orbach, 1978, 1986; Chernin,

1981; MacLeod, 1981; Lawrence, 1984; Wolf, 1990) in which the 'cultural' (Schwartz et al., 1985; Swartz, 1987; Nasser, 1988) and 'social' are commonly invoked, sociologists and social anthropologists have by and large not picked up the considerable analytic challenge they represent (but see Chapter 6). Commenting on this failure Hodes (1991) has recently proposed adopting the schema of the structure of meals presented by Douglas and Nicod (1974) as a potentially fruitful basis for investigating the extent to which the life-threatening avoidance of ingestion is evident in chaotic conceptions of meal patterning among anorexics.

Finally, beliefs and practices affecting the safety of food itself are remarkably under-researched, even in developing countries where the health-related problems are grave, extensive and well-known. As Foster and Kaferstein have succinctly observed: 'The study of conditions and customs that encourage unsafe food ... present no special research problems. The data are, so to speak, there for the asking or observing' (Foster and Kaferstein, 1985: 1274).

Such is the huge amount that has been written in recent years on eating disorders such as anorexia nervosa and bulimia, by doctors, psychiatrists, psychologists, historians and feminists as well as a handful of sociologists, that it is beyond the scope of this report to cover the literature fully. Nevertheless, we have skirted the topic in several sections, and will here mention some of the main issues relevant to the sociology of food and eating.

THE LONG-TERM CIVILISING OF APPETITE?

Medical historians have not been unanimous about whether the incidence of eating disorders is a characteristic exclusively of the last hundred years or so, or whether they have always existed. It is, however, undeniable that they have attracted far more attention in recent decades, and the balance of evidence now seems to support the view that this is not simply a matter of medical fashion but of a real increase in their incidence in the course of roughly the last hundred years (see Brumberg, 1988).

If this is so, the question arises of how the trend is to be explained. Mennell (1986a, 1987b; Mennell and Simons, 1989) has attempted to set it in the context of a broader long-term social process of changes in the control of appetite in the quantitative sense. The amount of food humans eat is not simply determined by biological factors, but is heavily influenced by cultural, social and psychological pressures. In European society since the Middle Ages a process of the 'civilising of appetite' (part of the overall civilising process identified by Elias) can be discerned in changing patterns of controls over appetite. They appear to have changed in the direction of more even and more all-embracing controls. To speak of 'more even' controls is to refer to a psychological change: the controls have come to operate in the average person in a

---

* This Chapter was written in collaboration with Dr Katherine Simons of the Department of Social Medicine, University of Birmingham Medical School, drawing on her PhD thesis (1990), and on Mennell and Simons (1989).

more automatic and regular way. By 'more all-embracing' is meant that there has also been a decline in behavioural differences between various spheres of social life; for instance, it may be that contrasts have diminished between behaviour acceptable in 'public' and 'private' life, or between normal occasions and special occasions such as carnivals when normal rules were temporarily abandoned.

In the Middle Ages, there were great inequalities in the social distribution of nourishment (see Mennell, 1985: 40–61), but in all social ranks there was an oscillating pattern of eating related to the insecurity of life in general, and of food supplies in particular. The pressures towards foresight and self-restraint were relatively weak and discontinuous. The problem of appetite in relation to over-abundant food had still scarcely arisen earlier than the eighteenth century for the great majority of people of western Europe; for them the most pressing external constraints on appetite were still the shortage or irregularity of food supplies. Until then, the upper classes often distinguished themselves from the lower by the sheer quantity of food they consumed. By the late seventeenth and the eighteenth centuries this was less easily possible, and social distinction came to be expressed more through the quality and refinement of cooking than through sheer quantitative stuffing. The change towards restraint of appetite began to be expressed in medical opinion in France and England (notably by Cheyne, 1724, 1733; cf. Turner, 1982a, 1982b). In the nineteenth century, the virtue of moderation and disdain for gluttony were increasingly stressed by bourgeois gastronomes, as a concern with obesity as a result of overeating began to be felt in well-to-do circles. Yet towards the end of the century, books and articles were still being addressed to lower-middle-class readers advising them on how to become plump, which shows that the ideal of the slim figure was not yet universal in European society. The problem and the fear of fatness gradually spread down the social scale, 'slimming' becoming a prominent concern in the popular press in the twentieth century. The social standards of expected self-control over appetite have developed so that they make much greater demands on individual people than formerly, and the growing incidence of eating disorders like anorexia and bulimia afflicting a minority appears to be related to these changes in social standards for the majority.

WHY WOMEN?

The eating disorder anorexia nervosa was recognised in the nineteenth century, and appears to represent one way in which a person may fail to acquire or may lose normal, relatively even and steady controls over appetite. Physiological regulating mechanisms are evidently disrupted by socially and psychologically induced extreme abstinence. Another syndrome associated with a morbid fear of fatness, but expressed through severe binge eating, combined with purging and self-induced vomiting and associated with a morbid fear of fatness, has attracted attention only in the last decade or thereabouts, and has been termed bulimia nervosa (Russell, 1979) or bulimia (American Psychiatric Association, *Diagnostic Statistical Manual*, vol. III, 1980)[6]. Although it is superficially different in its behavioural manifestation, Wardle and Beinart (1981) conclude that, like anorexia, 'binge eating is as much a consequence as a precipitant of dietary restriction.'

The main body of research into eating disorders has concentrated on the medical and psychological facets and neglects the social processes involved. The demographic distribution of eating disorders implies that sociocultural components play a larger part than the predominant focus of the research would suggest. Particularly affecting certain demographic groups, eating disorders are most prevalent in modern industrial countries among young, white, affluent women (Crisp, 1977; Willi and Grossman, 1983). Why?

Remarking on the substantial increase of eating disorders in the previous twenty years, Bruch (1978:8) observes that '... one might speak of an epidemic illness, only there is no contagious agent; the spread must be attributed to psycho-sociological factors. I am inclined to relate it to the enormous emphasis that Fashion places on slimness'. Garner et al. (1980) found a significant increase in the proportion of space given to material about diet and slimming in six major women's magazines between 1969 and 1979 compared with the previous ten years. They also studied *Playboy* magazine Playmate centrefolds, and contestants and winners of the Miss America Pageant from 1959 to 1978 as examples of ideal feminine beauty. In both groups of women they found that mean weights were significantly less than corresponding population means published by the Society of Actuaries for each year. In addition, within each of the two groups, weight declined across the twenty-year period which was studied. Therefore, not only were those women selected as ideal body types consistently thinner than the actual means for comparable women in the population, but also these

---

[6] The disorder made its first appearance in the American Psychiatric Association's *DSM* in the 1980 edition.

ideal body types became thinner over time. These findings cannot be explained simply as a reflection of a decrease in average body weights over the twenty-year period, because the comparison of actuarial norms from 1959 with those of 1979 show that the average weight of women under thirty (the age group from which *Playboy* playmates and Miss America contestants are most likely to come) is consistently several pounds heavier in 1979 than in 1959. In other words, the average weight of the population is increasing at the same time that pressures to be slim are growing and the size of the ideal body image is diminishing.

Many explanations for the profound importance of a slim physique have been offered. Most tend to focus on the aesthetics of physique, personality traits associated with physique, and behaviour inferred from physique. Thinness is not only presented as attractive but associated with success, power and other highly valued attributes. Being overweight, on the other hand, is considered physically and morally unhealthy, 'obscene', 'lazy', 'slothful' and 'gluttonous' (Dejong, 1980; Ritenbaugh, 1982; Schwartz et al., 1982). The positive and negative evaluations of physique are extended by inference to typical patterns of correlated behaviour and moral attributes: self-control and self-indulgence respectively. While all this may be true, in our view it is secondary to an explanation of the slimness ideal in terms of social competition. It was only relatively recently, in the space of the last hundred years, that the majority of the people of industrial societies acquired the means and opportunity to become plump. When they did so, it would then follow a very typical pattern if the upper strata chose to distinguish themselves from their inferiors by adopting an ideal of slimness, which in turn would be emulated by the middle classes, and so on. (Significantly, recent reports suggest that the incidence of anorexia is rising faster among women in lower social strata than those where it has hitherto been most common; see Garfinkel and Garner, 1982, and especially the various studies they cite on p. 103).

In view of the historical shift towards the preference for thinness it is not suprising that more women than at any other time are becoming increasingly preoccupied with their weight and size and routinely plagued by food. Research has established that the majority of women in Western culture – probably as many as between 80 and 90 percent (Button and Whitehouse, 1981) constantly monitor their daily calorie intake and eat less than is required to stop them feeling hungry. In a social climate in which thinness is synonymous with female beauty, the majority of women report that they would like to be thinner and attempt to restrict their food intake in response to social pressures.

There is reason to believe that what today constitutes 'normal' eating is not entirely appropriate to physiological needs. Polivy and Herman (1987) argue that what is regarded as socially normal eating actually displays many characteristics of the abnormal eating habits identified in eating disorders, and may itself be regarded as disordered or pathological. For example, many of the symptoms reported by bulimic patients are also commonly reported by those in the general population (Cooper and Fairburn, 1983; Hart and Ollendick, 1985). Meadows et al. (1986) carried out a survey of the eating habits of women aged between 18 and 22 registered with the doctors of one general practice. As many as 11.6 percent of the women reported that they 'often' ate lots of fattening foods in binges. These findings suggest that bulimic behaviour is unusual only in the more extreme *degree* to which patterns common to people at large (for a very broad overview see Chapter 7) become evident in bulimia sufferers.

It could be argued, then, that while eating disorders have attracted much attention from women psychotherapists such as Hilde Bruch (1973, 1978; cf. Turner, 1990, 1991; Horsfall, 1991), Carol Bloom (1987) and Striegel-Moore et al. (1986), sociologists should be more interested in them as an extreme symptom of social pressures on people, especially women, more generally. The greater pressure for thinness among women than among men has been clearly demonstrated through empirical research. For example, Fallon and Rozin (1985) found that college women perceive their own figures to be heavier than the figure they consider most attractive to men, and their ideal figure to be thinner still. In contrast, college men display no difference in perceptions of their own figure, their ideal figure and the figure they consider most attractive to women.

Several writers have analysed the pattern of female socialisation seemingly implicated in these differences. Passivity, compliance and selflessness are encouraged in girls while boys are expected to be independent, active and assertive. Lawrence (1984) suggests that although girls might have equal opportunities to boys in education, they are not prepared for the experience of work success and independence: 'All girls are socialised into a sexual identity centred on motherhood, regardless of whether or not they later also have the opportunity to achieve educational success and make their own careers.' In general boys are socialised into careers while girls are socialised into carers. The link between the process of socialisation and unusual eating behaviour is confirmed by studies which show that self-reported binge eating tendencies and low self-esteem, rigid dieting and negative body image are found not only in clinical samples but in the general population, and in women more often than men. Boskind-Lohdahl (1976) is able to conclude that 'Bulimarexia is not a psychiatric problem but reflects a problem of female socialisation'. Palazolli (1974) describes the 'contradictory roles and expectations made of young women' in modern society, and the 'ridicule and rejection of fat women'; Minuchin (1978) blames the patriarchal society and notes the 'irony' of the increasing prevalence of eating disorders in the face of women's dawning emancipation.

It has been suggested that it is no coincidence that an increase in the prevalence of eating disorders has occurred simultaneously with the rise of the feminist movement. The argument turns on the following: the once acceptable role of motherhood and the sense of fulfilment gained from the experience has been the target of feminist propaganda. Women are informed that caring for a family is mundane and demeaning; they are encouraged to assert themselves and realise their potential in their own right, outside their home and family. However, conflict may be experienced between 'feminine' values, only partly rejected if at all in the domestic sphere and in seeking a sexual partner, and the essentially more assertive, 'masculine' style necessary to succeed in other spheres. Susie Orbach (1986: 28) describes women who enter the world beyond the home as 'guests ... [who] must conform to prevailing masculinist values and accept entry on that basis'.

Thus women are placed in an ambiguous and contradictory situation. Against a background of traditional feminine values which emphasize compliance, passivity and dependency, opportunities and choices arise for vocational success and achievement. These entail independence, ambition and assertiveness. Hilde Bruch (1978) suggests that increased opportunities for women may be experienced as excessive demands. Attempts to meet the demands and reconcile the differences between the traditional and the feminist ideologies, make it difficult for women to feel secure in whichever role they decide to adopt.

Addressing the changing roles of women, Chernin (1986) describes the present 'unique generation of women – the first in history to have the social and psychological opportunity to surpass with ease the life choice our mothers have made'. She maintains that:

> ... the recent epidemic of eating disorders must be understood as a profound development crisis in a generation of women still deeply confused, after twenty years of struggle for female liberation, about what it means to be a woman in the modern world, that is the problem of taking on the rights and prerogatives of male society. (Chernin, 1986: 12)

Patterns of Food Consumption

In broad terms, food consumption is patterned in association with some of the main 'key variables' of social accounting in industrialised nations, namely social class, age and sex. These patterns are revealed repeatedly in data collected routinely for such practical purposes as market research or the compilation of official statistics on food consumption, and they show patterns persisting over and above poverty, want or scarcity. They form the pre-sociological baseline for explanations of social and cultural bases for the social distribution of 'choice', 'habit' or 'taste' with which much of this report is concerned. This section briefly establishes their contours and sketches the scope for fuller sociological investigation.

CLASS

Higher socio-economic groups are generally reported to consume a greater range and variety of foodstuffs which are more likely to accord with the nutritionally approved orthodoxy of the day, than those lower down the social scale (MAFF Annual 1951– ; Gregory et al., 1990). As the widely adopted dietary guidelines of the 1980s recommended a reduction in the intake of salt, sugar and (saturated) fat, and an increase in the consumption of dietary fibre, so a class-gradient is observed in the use of items such as skimmed milk, vegetables and brown bread. Fruit provides a particularly clear example of foods currently highly recommended for the maintenance of good health. Its consumption is commonly observed to be greater in the higher income/professional groups – in, for example, Denmark (Haraldsdottir, 1987); Northern Ireland (Barker et al., 1988); England and Wales (Blaxter, 1990); and Finland (Helminen and Prättälä, 1990). Similarly, diets with higher amounts of animal fat are more likely to be recorded among lower socio-economic groups (Blaxter, 1990, Barker et al., 1988) and among farmers, e.g. in Finland (Prättälä and Helminen, 1990), Switzerland (Gex-Fabry et al., 1988) and France (Grignon and Grignon, 1981).

Such class variations are evident in other forms of food consumption.

Middle-class infants are more likely to be breast-fed, as currently medically advised, than those born to working-class parents in industrialised societies (Martin, 1978) – a phenomenon also reported in developing countries, though class is often encoded in the use of terms such as industrialisation, poverty or urbanisation (e.g. Thomas, 1981; Underwood and Margetts, 1987; Dettwyler, 1987; Manderson, 1984). Levenstein (1988) suggests that the upper and middle classes are responsible for a disproportionately great share of the nearly 20 percent of the total spent on retail foods in the USA which goes on special 'reduced' or 'diet' foods. And in Britain (Fiddes, 1991), the Netherlands and probably most other industrialised countries it is the middle classes that are more likely to be vegetarian. Cooking methods also show a class gradient – frying rather than baking or grilling being more common among lower socio-economic groups. Smaller-scale studies reveal that class variations in consumption patterns are finely grained. Calnan (1990) reports that working-class households in Britain are more likely to have purchased tinned and frozen rather than fresh vegetables (as well as white bread, white flour, full-fat milk and more sugar) than those in the middle class. Ekström (1991), however, reports no class differences in vegetable consumption in Swedish families, but a greater likelihood that the middle classes take alcohol at meals.

SEX

Overall, females are reported to consume smaller total amounts of food than do men. Differences in average stature and, in part, energy expenditure, cannot be discounted (Department of Health, 1991; Gregory et al., 1990) but they do not wholly account for the differentials in consumption patterns reported.

Sex differences in consumption of amount and type of food are widely found to be bolstered by accompanying beliefs, taboos, cultural prescriptions and proscriptions in different eras and in different societies (Delphy, 1979; Odebiyi, 1989; Swantz, 1975; O'Laughlin, 1974; de Garine and Koppert, 1990) though they may not always be followed in practice (Manderson, 1981). For instance, Chapman (1990) reports a marked distinction between the food and drink typically consumed by men and women in a Brittany fishing village. Pork paté, sausage and fat, with white bread, are considered characteristically masculine, while women take cake made of white flour and butter. Correspondingly, where women drink great quantities of coffee, men drink an awesome amount of red wine – taken as 'virtually their entire daily fluid intake, after the morning bowl of coffee. Two litres a day is normal. Five is not unknown' (Chapman, 1990: 32). Men regard wine as good for the blood, strong and red as masculine blood should be. It is contrasted to milk, white and feeble, held to be a child's or woman's drink that is positively bad for the adult masculine digestion and health.

In the North East of England, beer consumption marks distinctions between men and women in similar fashion. This is the region in which allegiance to ale, as distinct from the increasingly ubiquitous lager, remains strong. And it is men who sustain this allegiance, maintaining that the palate has to be developed. And a palate for ale is held to be an exclusively male attribute. Lager is for women (and ill-tutored youngsters). Learning to appreciate ale is a process that can effectively only take place in those bastions of English maleness, pubs and working men's clubs (Gofton, 1983).

Critical of discriminatory beliefs, Shapiro (1986) sees a historical continuity. Women, she claims, are still 'haunt[ed] by what Miss Sedgwick, a mid-nineteenth century New England moralist, described as the "monster appetite"'. And she tartly recalls an observation of 1903 that 'lunch was of no interest to a *normal* woman' (Shapiro, 1986: 233; emphasis added). Though less likely to be overweight than men in, for example, the USA, the Netherlands, Canada, Australia, Finland and Great Britain (Rissanen et al., 1988), women are more likely than men to reduce their food intake as a means of achieving weight loss. Adolescent girls are found more likely than boys of the same age to endorse statements that most people need to lose weight (Hamblin, 1980). In Northern Ireland, 12.6 percent of the women sampled but only 2.3 percent of the men described themselves as on a weight-controlling diet (Barker et al., 1988). And (see Chapter 6) it is well known that eating disorders, (especially those entailing self-starvation and self-administered purging) have increased among females to a far greater extent than among males over the last few decades (Farmer et al., 1986). How far some hint of a distinctive attitude to food prevails among women and is at issue when they seek to interpret possible alterations in appetite associated with pregnancy (Murcott, 1988b) requires further investigation.

Meat avoidance generally is reported to be more common nowadays among women than men, with half of all British women claiming to be 'eating less meat' (Fiddes, 1991: 29). According to Bourdieu, in France at least, these differences in consumption run much deeper than at first appears:

... the whole body schema, in particular the physical approach to the act of eating, governs the selection of certain food. For example, in the working classes, fish tends to be regarded as an unsuitable food for men, not only because it is light food, insufficiently 'filling', ... but also because, like fruit (except bananas) it is one of the 'fiddly' things which a man's hands cannot cope with and which make him childlike (the woman, adopting a maternal role, ... will prepare the fish on the plate or peel the pear); but above all, it is because fish has to be eaten in a way which totally contradicts the masculine way of eating, that is, with restraint, in small mouthfuls, chewed gently ... (because of the bones). The whole masculine identity – what is called virility – is involved in these two ways of eating: nibbling or picking, as befits a woman, or with wholehearted male gulps and mouthfuls .... (1979: 190–1)

Cross-cut with class, Charles and Kerr (1988) report a notable difference in the consumption of more expensive cuts of red meat such that the working-class men of their sample consumed greater amounts than middle-class men, whereas little class difference was evident among the women.

In industrialised nations, sex differences in food consumption may have few gross implications for health in the population as a whole. Elsewhere, however, sex distinctions in consumption can have far graver and more immediately obvious consequences. In South Asia, for instance, Sen (1985) has commented on a sharp 'bias' against women in the distribution of food. The association with gender differences in mortality, morbidity and malnutrition in that region is inescapable (Harriss, 1990).

AGE

Sociologically, age only surfaces as anything more than a convention-ally collected datum (Finch, 1987) when calendar years signify social and/or biological capacity, maturity or infirmity in implied comparison with 'normal' adulthood. In this sense, infants and the elderly occupy similar social locations both to one another and to the sick and mentally retarded. Food consumption practices and beliefs provide one arena in which this cultural location can be made apparent (see Murcott, forthcoming b).

Compared with the burgeoning mass of research on the relation of food consumption and eating patterns to sex, which is partly the product of the upsurge of feminist sociology, sociological work on food among the elderly in industrialised nations is relatively less developed. The sociology of ageing, however, is a distinctive and well funded field in the USA. McIntosh and his associates have published a number of papers arising from a large-scale empirical survey in this area (McIntosh and Shifflett, 1984; Shifflett and McIntosh, 1986; McIntosh, 1988; McIntosh et al., 1989). The main thrust of this research centres of the hypothesised tendency of old people, especially when living alone, recently widowed, or in indifferent health, to neglect their diet and suffer consequential nutritional deterioration. McIntosh and his associates have explored how eating habits are affected by the social support which involvement in social networks (including religious organisations) gives to the elderly, and by whether an elderly person has a long or short perspective of future time.

In Europe, a gap appears to remain at the moment, but is very likely to be filled in the near future as the eating habits and needs of the elderly become one of the major targets for research. On the one hand there is a continuing policy focus on the old age as constituting a period of life at nutritional risk (see, e.g., Flint, 1982, for Australia). On the other, there are newly developing studies of the material, social circumstances of the elderly in an 'ageist' context (Arber and Ginn, 1991) together with some attention to the household focus of gendered power relationships and the domestic division of labour (Mason, 1987) (see Chapter 12 on Food Preparation in the Division of Labour at Home).

Youth, however, is a rather different matter. Good nutrition in the early years of life is held to contribute to securing a healthy adulthood (Pelto, 1987, Darke, 1980). This bio-medical assumption shades over and is consonant with predominant Western ideologies of childhood, which are continually characterised in terms of the future (James and Prout, 1990). In food consumption as in anything else, it is widely assumed that 'habits' 'behaviour' and 'preferences' acquired in childhood shape those of adulthood – creating patterns that are resistant to change. Socio-medical surveillance of children and their caretakers inevitably includes concern with the manner in which they are fed – a concern so self-evidently worthy that moralising does not always need to be concealed. The history of infant feeding is replete with examples (De Mause, 1974: 34). In turn, feeding babies and children is only too readily characterised as a problem that has become 'medicalised' (Fischler, 1986a, 1986b).

While the social policing of children is the subject of sociological (and historical) investigation, it is also, of course, the ideological source creating the rationale (as well, it may be supposed, as funding opportunities) for research (Fink, 1985). Such work has as often been undertaken by nutritionists and public health experts as by social scientists (for recent examples worldwide, see Truswell and Darnton-Hill,

1981; King and Ashworth, 1987; Tucker and Sanjur, 1988; Shack et al., 1990; Doan and Bisharat, 1990). In Britain, infant feeding practices are the subject of public health inspired monitoring (Martin, 1978). Research on food consumption in the early years of life focuses prominently on influences leading to artificial- rather than breast-feeding and the introduction of mixed feeding. This work includes study of the impact of commercial activity and advertising, especially in developing countries (Hung et al., 1985; Igun, 1982), the relation to social networks (for instance among different ethnic groups in Florida: Bryant, 1982), the association with women's status within the household (in Jordan: Doan and Bisharat, 1990) and in Britain the influence of maternal attitudes (Jones, 1986).

Implicitly this rationale extends to assumptions that children's eating habits are unexceptionable topics for investigation. The documentation of secular changes in life-style formed the mainspring for Prättälä's (1989) combined sociological and nutritional investigation of teenagers' food consumption patterns in Finland. Adolescents are confronted with a duality: well aware of the 'real' food of their parents and of nutritional advice on low fat and sugar consumption, they nonetheless find 'junk' food far more appealing. She shows that teenagers 'manage' this duality according to social context: at home or with teachers they eat 'real' foods, but in company with peers opt for 'junk'. Popkin and Lim-Ybanez (1982) apply the economist's cast of mind to assessing the impact of nutrition on investments in education – they too assume that child feeding is self-evidently important.

In Britain, changes in government policy on school-meal provision in the early 1980s provided the occasion for specially mounted monitoring of children's diets (Murcott, 1987; and for a historian's view more widely, see Welshman, 1986). The results suggest a modicum of cause for nutritional concern for schoolgirls' low intake of iron and all children's over-consumption of fat and sugar (Wenlock et al., 1986). And, as sociologists would expect, the higher the parental social class, the taller the children (using height as a proxy measure of the quality and quantity of nutritional intake). The report also records a small but suggestive finding that foreshadows a call in Chapter 13 for greater attention to the internal social organisation of the household and its relation to the distribution of food: 'Boys who were the only child in one-parent families appeared to have higher intakes of energy and most nutrients than boys who were the only child in two-parent families' (Wenlock et al., 1986: iv).

Data useful to sociologists on patterns of food consumption in the population is widely scattered in market research (see Allen, 1968, for Britain) and government reports. Much of the material discussed in Chapter 4 on Nutritional Trends, can be used in this context too. One particular gap, the study of elderly people's eating habits in the context of their life-styles and social networks, seems likely to be filled in the near future, since a number of projects are being funded in various countries.

Under this heading comes a vast field of research, historical, anthropological and sociological. The three polarities of shortage and plenty, fasting and feasting, and poverty and wealth are intimately related, for they all have to do with the quantity of food to which different groups of people at a certain time have access. Material wealth implies the possession of all sorts of goods, including plenty of food, which can easily be given away on the occasion of feasts. Poverty very often means a shortage of food which in turn will include fasting and hunger by coercive external circumstances. Voluntary fasting (aside from the religious and ascetic) is often restricted to individuals and groups living in affluence, including an abundant food supply: otherwise one has no choice.

The availability of food is influenced in the first place by the processes of production and distribution. A stable food supply in a country, resulting from a flourishing system of food production will, however, not always ensure the accessibility of a sufficient quantity to every group in the population. The organisation of food distribution, including markets, prices and networks, shapes the opportunities or obstacles to people's eating sufficient quantities of food. Feasts often form an opportunity for the redistribution of food; they still play a major role in Third World communities today (Douglas, 1984b). We shall glance very briefly at the oscillating process of long-term change from want to plenty which has taken place in Western countries over the last five centuries. This change, however, is not unilinear; poverty and want have returned for some groups or nations today, or have never been succesfully overcome.

FROM SHORTAGE TO PLENTY IN PAST AND PRESENT

In the history of western Europe, as in most other parts of the world, periods of shortage have alternated with periods of plenty. However, if we contrast the food situation in the Middle Ages, for instance, with that at present, it is clear that a general change has taken place which is characterised by a greatly increased security of the supply (Mennell, 1987a). This change, roughly, came about through the post-Columbian metamorphosis in the trade routes and the import of food crops, through the agrarian and industrial revolutions in general and the accompanying revolutions in agriculture, means of food transport, and food preservation (Van Otterloo, 1990). At the same time the general availability of food has been enlarged; processes of (functional, not necessarily political) democratisation during the past two centuries have ensured a more equal distribution of the accessibility of food to the population by the mechanism of wages (which went up) and prices (which went down).

Historians like Wilhelm Abel (1974) and Fernand Braudel (1979) have described mass poverty and crises of hunger in Europe roughly between 1400 and 1800, the centuries stretching from the waning of the Middle Ages to the eve of the Industrial Revolution. Burnett (1966) studied the diets of the different social groups of the population in England – the rich, including 'high society' and the prosperous middle classes, and the poor working-class families in the countryside as well as in the city. Burnett focused on changes in the diet of these classes during the last two centuries. These historians are only three of the best-known of a list of writers on the topic of contrasts between 'luxury and necessity' in the past and on problems of Western food shortage, famines and hunger. A great deal of this type of research is of a social and economic character, and restricts itself mainly to the 'supply-side' of food history (see Mennell, 1986a: 7–10; and Van Otterloo 1990: 302–10). Part of this literature is informed by nutritional knowledge (Oddy and Miller, 1976); Scrimshaw (1983) explicitly demonstrates its relevance for historians.

A topic often considered in this context is hunger revolts, as set in comparative perspective by Löwe (1986) in his study of France, England and Germany in the eighteenth century. A special branch of this type of historical research consists in assessing the demographical impact of famines, often in relation to epidemic diseases. Since Malthus's essay on the principles of population (1798), this subject has remained heavily debated by demographers and historians, amongst whose writings McKeown's (1977) theory of the decisive influence of food is very well known. Some of these authors focus on a specific time and place, such as Post (1985), while others aim at more generalised conclusions. In a study based on calculations and long-term historical data Watkins and Menken (1985) conclude that famines did not play a major role in accounting for long-term population stability.

The distinguished economist Amartya Sen has had a profound influence on the study of hunger since the publication of his book *Poverty and Famines* (1981), already mentioned in the introductory section above. Sen advanced a socio-economic model to elucidate the causes of hunger, mainly in the contemporary Third World. His explanation centres on systems of what he calls 'exchange entitlement' of what a person owns. 'A person will be exposed to starvation if, for the ownership that he actually has, the exchange entitlement set does not contain any feasible bundle [of commodities] including enough food' (1981: 3). He posits that starvation and famine are therefore not in the first place the outcome of instability and shortages of food supply. Hunger, on the contrary, is much more dependent on entitlements and ownership patterns prevailing in the community. This thesis, which Sen illuminated with several case studies, has been central to a whole broadly developing approach to problems of poverty, food-supply and famine by historians and other scholars, who have broken the bounds of time, space and discipline in the manner first demonstrated by Abel (1974) and Braudel (1979). Pfister (1988) stresses in his review article the importance of this interdisciplinary approach to issues of food supply and hunger both in the historical past and today.

This interdisciplinary approach to historical and contemporary problems of hunger is manifest in two recent volumes edited by Rotberg and Rabb (1985) and by Newman et al. (1990). The former brings together essays by historians, social scientists and food scientists, covering the different forms of scarcity at various times and in all continents of the world. One of the contributors, Tilly (1985), discusses the redistribution of food entitlements in England and France; the rise of capitalism and the development of the nation-state, she shows, were the main factors contributing to these changes. Newman's volume covers four time periods: the age of early humans (hunter-gatherers through to the beginnings of agriculture); the development of urban centres beginning a few millennia ago; the development of a world-wide economic system over the last few centuries; and the emergence of a global food-system in the recent past. Newman's range of contributing disciplines is even wider, including also geography, geology and linguistics. Sen himself contributes a paper on food entitlements and economic chains; looking to the future of hunger he concludes 'that its diminution and perhaps even its demise may be *attainable* [but is] surely not guaranteed' (Sen, 1990: 403–4). Of all the conditions and changes needed to attain this goal, one is most important: 'to include the excluded, the marginal people and places constituting the bulk of the world's hungry (1990: 406).

Sorokin (1975 [orig. 1922]) and Obregón (1985) by contrast concentrate on famines in specific countries, Russia and Spain respectively. Pitirim Sorokin is one of the very few sociologists to have written on this subject very systematically. He provides an extensive analysis of the social and individual consequences of the great famine in his country (1919–21). In such circumstances human behaviour is finally reduced to the search for food. Thus, according to him, there is a direct relationship between people's food situation and the character of their relationships (see also Chapter 1). Peter Garnsey (1990) studied famine and food supply in the classical Græco-Roman world. Food crises were a frequent event in antiquity, but that was not true of famines. As a specialist in ancient history, the author focuses on the survival strategies of the peasantry and of urban communities, and especially on the responses to risk and crisis. City governments did very little to guarantee the regularity of food supplies, while the rich elite practised 'euergetism' (public generosity), though not without self-interest. Garnsey concludes that:

> Food crisis was endemic in the Mediterranean in classical antiquity. Its origins lay in nature and in man, often operating together. Harvest failure was an underlying cause of food shortage. However, food crisis was the consequence of a sharp reduction, not in the absolute level of food supply, but in food availability. The causes of famine are to be sought not only in the physical environment and conditions of production, but also in distribution mechanisms, their limitations, and their disruption through human intervention. (1990: 271)

In contemporary pre-industrial or partly industrialised developing countries the food supply is still not stabilised. For this reason a great many studies deal with problems of widespread shortage and hunger in these regions. Boserup (1983), for instance, discusses the influence of scarcity and plenty on development; she concludes that the interrelationship between these factors is much more complicated than neo-Malthusian theories assume. The advantages of technological change are never shared equally by all population groups; 'rapid growth of the population and rapid growth of per capita income go together with malnutrition and sometimes starvation among the poor' (pp. 208–9). Moore (1990) introduces another angle; the concept of famine appears not to mean the same thing for Western and Third World peoples. The last-mentioned define famine as a situation of poverty and powerlessness, an inability to avoid destitution. Other aspects of the world food problem which have to do with power and powerlessness, politics and policies are also critically discussed from different perspectives in many different interdisciplinary journals. (Douglas, 1984a; Johnson, 1986; George, 1986; Whit, 1988).

FASTING AND FEASTING

The contrast between fasting and feasting is, according to Mennell (1987a), connected with alternating periods of shortage and plenty which were characteristic of the instability of food supplies during the Middle Ages. Wealthy elite groups tried to impress others of equal rank and especially people of poor status with ostentatious and lavish feasting, banqueting and the consumption of huge quantities of food. On the other side of the societal gap between high and low, rich and poor, scanty and monotonous meals were the norm. This is a general polarity which is often recognised, described and interpreted, for instance by Goody (1982) who made the contrast between high and low culinary culture to his central theme. In this study he does not restrict himself to societal classes in one society but he stretches his analysis unto the comparison of the continents of Eurasia and Africa (see Chapter 2 on the Development of Culinary Cultures).

Fasting can be coercive because of poor economic conditions, or it can be elective as in the case of a religious belief. Feasting in modern Western countries has kept its social functions of expressing and initiating ties of kinship, friendship and neighbourhood. Eating and sharing of food and drink remain important for these reasons, but not as means of redistribution of food to those people who otherwise do not have enough. Feasting, however, continues to have this function of redistribution in developing countries. Here forms of hospitality (inclusive or exclusive) restrict or open up possibilities to add to the scanty fare of larger or smaller segments of the local population (Douglas, 1984a). The insufficient food supply and the unequal distribution of entitlements to food, continue to shape the functioning of patterns of hospitality.

FOOD AND SOCIAL INEQUALITY: OLD AND NEW DEPRIVATION IN CONTEMPORARY WESTERN COUNTRIES

Apart from the general food supply, which can be disturbed by crop-failure or other natural or human disasters like wars, the problem of the distribution of food is at least as important. Plenty and want throughout history have never been distributed equally within the population. The condition of differential accessibility of food has to do with the power relationships between the social strata in a country. In modern market economies, this is always a question of having scarce or lavish financial means to spend. The quantity of income available is dependent on other characteristics of social stratification like education and occupation. Incomes in Western countries have in general greatly increased, especially since the Second World War; with the increase in income, the fraction of expenditure on food has decreased, as the Belgian statistician Quételet had already observed in the last century. Nevertheless, in the last decades new groups afflicted with poverty in the midst of plenty, because of economic crisis and unemployment, have been re-discovered (Harrington, 1963; Coates and Silburn, 1970, 1983). Especially in the United States, this is a widespread problem (Brown, 1987; Fitchen, 1988), but it is by no means absent elsewhere (Driver, 1984).

Part of the work on these problems refers to the topic of social inequality relating to food and health, which has remained or which has arisen anew between rich and poor groups in modern society (see, for Britain, Townsend and Davidson, 1982; Whitehead, 1988). Poverty and resultant food shortage (real or possible) among underprivileged groups in contemporary Western countries are a recurring subject of study (Townsend, 1979). The return to widespread poverty for some groups has caused the initiation of several assistance programmes and other measures, which are accompanied by sociological and nutritional research. Petchers, Chow and Kordish (1989), for instance, interviewed clients of urban Emergency Food Centres, a modern variety of the nineteenth-century soup-kitchens. They found that hunger remained a problem even among those who made use of the food centres. DeVault and Pitts (1984), Cohen (1987), and Basiotis et al. (1987) did research on, respectively, the origins, the legislative aspects and the nutrititional consequences of the American Food Stamps Program (1987), which is one of the results of the national debate on hunger that has taken place in the USA since the 1960s. Although the food intake and the nutritional status of the diet of low income families participating in the programme improved, this is, according to DeVault and Pitts, only a partial solution to the problem, because it diverts attention from the social conditions which produce hunger.

Another stream of research on the general theme of shortage and plenty is the study of food habits, beliefs and practices in lower status groups, contrasted with higher status groups – another variation on the theme of 'high and low' (see for instance Grignon and Grignon, 1981; Grignon,1986).Inspiteoffar-reachingprocessesofdemocratisationinmeans and ways of living and eating, different social strata seem always to keep some characteristic practices and preferences at table (Bourdieu, 1979). Contemporary examples verifying the inverse relationship between expenditure on food and overall income – established in the 1850s by Ernst Engel and known as 'Engel's Law' – are mentioned by Herpin (1984). Engel posited that the level of expenditure on food rose in proportion to income; in testing this regularity, Herpin points to a second possibility, that increasing income is also accompanied by a falling consumption of 'inferior' products in favour of those of 'higher' quality. (This possibility was also discovered in the nineteenth century by the English economist Robert Giffen; 'inferior' goods are also known among economists as 'Giffen goods'.) Herpin shows that this in fact happens among modern city dwellers, and that in this respect urban workers' typical shopping baskets are as varied as those of other social categories. What city dwellers get to eat, he contends, is more highly dependent on the household's demographic and economic position, and much less on socio-cultural factors than Bourdieu implies.

9

Food Technology and Its Impact

Modern food technology has had a tremendous impact on Western societies and even on world society as a whole. This impact is felt across the whole range of production, distribution, preparation and consumption which constitute the main phases in the social role of food (Goody, 1982: 37). Yet food technology is as old as human food production and preparation. It started with the hunters and gatherers' invention and improvement of techniques for extracting a livelihood from the wilderness. Later, agriculturalists and stock-breeders developed techniques for sedentary crop growing and dairying; they also invented several ways of conserving their food surpluses. Examples are the making of curds, yogurt, cheese and butter, and the smoking, drying and salting of meat and fish. This millennia-long, slow but steady growth in technical knowledge and capacity to ensure stable food supply underwent a sudden acceleration with the arrival of the industrial era. In the nineteenth century, the industrialisation of food production (on the farm as well as in the factory) began in several European countries, and similar societies such as the USA and Australia. One of the most important incentives in this process was the rapid development of scientific knowledge based on international competition and conflict (Farrer, 1980; Van Otterloo, 1990: 54–9; Sorj and Wilkinson, 1985: 302).

INDUSTRIALISATION OF AGRICULTURAL AND ARTISAN FOOD PRODUCTION

Industrial food on a somewhat larger scale is of comparatively recent origin: it dates back little more than a century. After 1800, new developments in the sciences of chemistry, biology and physiology led to various types of specialisation and especially to the beginnings of the sciences of nutrition and microbiology. These and other developments opened up the possibility of knowing the exact composition of foodstuffs and about the micro-processes which lead to their growth and decay. Mechanisation encountered the organic: tractors, artificial fertilisers and pesticides structurally changed agriculture ensuring much larger harvests (Giedion, 1975: 130). Techniques of food processing and preservation, already improved by trial and error like the invention of sterilisation by Nicolas Appert, could now be perfected. In several Western countries – England, Denmark, The Netherlands, the United States, with favourable market conditions and no strong tradition of peasant farming – these scientific developments, combined with rapidly expanding mechanisation on the basis of new energy sources, led to the establishment of giant food companies. Here the farm and artisan production of flour and bread, the preservation of meat and vegetables and the making of butter and cheese were quickly replaced by milling, baking, canning (later followed by freezing) and milk and dairying industries. Margarine, of course, was the greatest early triumph of food industrialisation (Stuyvenberg, 1969), perhaps followed by beet-sugar (Goody, 1982: 154–74; Oddy and Miller, 1976; Sorj and Wilkinson, 1985; Teuteberg and Wiegelmann, 1986).

The developments in agricultural and food technologies and the rise of food companies in the nineteenth century have been described not so much by sociologists as by historians. The same is true for the changes in distribution, preparation and consumption dealt with below. A famous example is Charles Wilson's (1954) history of Unilever: a popular history of the industrialisation of food is that by Tannahill (1973).

DISTRIBUTION

The technological changes in production and processing implied a restructuring and massive increase in the size of markets for foodstuffs made possible and stimulated by the improvement of the means of transport and the widespread processes of urbanisation (Teuteberg, 1987; Levenstein, 1988; Van Otterloo, 1990). Another consequence of the growth of food technology, in conjunction with centralisation and bureaucratisation, was the enactment of laws against food adulteration. In the last quarter of the nineteenth and the first decades of the twentieth century this happened – frequently after long drawn out power struggles between different interest groups – in most of the Western states (Ellerbrock, 1987: 127–89; Teuteberg and Wiegelmann, 1986; Winkler, 1985; Paulus, 1974). A third implication was the growth of an extended retailing system of various types of food shops by which a variety of foodstuffs (often weighed and packed) were made available to the new citizens; this system took the place of the old open market (Oddy and Miller, 1976; Teuteberg and Wiegelmann, 1986: 163–84).

PREPARATION AND CONSUMPTION

The restructuring of life embedded in the more general social process of industrialisation has had far-reaching consequences for meals and meal patterns, as did the industrialisation of foodstuff production. The time, the number, the composition and the temperature (hot or cold) of meals changed during the process of transformation from agricultural and artisan societies to industrial and urban ones. Teuteberg and Wiegelmann (1972, 1986) studied a range of such changes in Germany and other parts of Central Europe, Crawford and Broadley (1938), Oddy and Miller (1976) did so in England, Den Hartog (1980) and Van Otterloo (1990) in the Netherlands, Levenstein (1988) in the United States, and Rotenberg (1981) in Austria.

A most general effect of the industrialisation of food production and the reorganisation of trade networks was the end of widespread hunger and scarcity. At the turn of the century more food than ever was available, and by 1950 shortages in Western industrialised countries for the lower economic strata and their consequences for health were over. More specifically, improved food technology meant the availability of substitutes such as beet-sugar and margarine, and new food products, ready for use, developed from their origins in earlier centuries into a proliferation of new versions for twentieth-century mass markets: dehydrated potato and maize-flour, evaporated milk, biscuits, cornflakes and other breakfast cereals, tinned meat, fish and fruits. All of these products changed the plight of the kitchen-maid and the housewife. Preparation of food at home was also made easier when open fires were replaced by gas or electric stoves (improved still further by the introduction in the first half of this century of thermostatic controls) and piped water in houses and kitchens became nearly universal (Schwarz-Cowan, 1983; Strasser, 1982). Urbanisation and the geographical separation of the home and the workplace led people to change their eating habits: bread, cereals and coffee or tea in the morning instead of porridge, ham or bacon and eggs, baked potatoes or pancakes; the hot meal at noon was postponed till the evening, and lunch came to resemble breakfast, at least in northern Europe and the United States. In countries such as France and Italy the hot meal at noon was more widely maintained. A most important implication of food technology and the quantitative and qualitative change in food supply (combined with rising incomes), was the considerable rise in the consumption of (high-energy) meat and dairy products, and the use of a larger variety of foodstuffs.

RECENT DEVELOPMENTS IN FOOD TECHNOLOGY

After 1950, with peace and rising affluence, new waves of technological applications in the field of food followed one another at increasing speed (see Pyke, 1970, 1972). 'Product innovation' is the motor behind this ongoing development, which also is tightly bound to economic circumstances. The ingredients of new foodstuffs are more and more derived by synthetic means, which makes them less recognisable as original products of the farm. The growth of technology and – since the 1980s – of biotechnology applied to plants and animals has been substantial. Their implications for the production, distribution and preparation of food can be summarised in the following tendencies:

The rise of agribusiness and other global food networks

Internationalisation of food companies and food markets began through the need for raw materials, for instance vegetable oils and fats for the production of margarine. However, whereas earlier methods of food processing and manufacture started from primary agricultural products, the growth of the food industry has increasingly come to be driven by the demands of industrial processes and world markets. Agriculture has become dependent on industry; this has led to the rise of giant agribusiness firms which frequently have taken over plantations and factories in primary producing tropical and sub-tropical countries. Critics of these trends point to the unintended effects of the existence of these transnational corporations, most of them established in the 1970s, which often amount to the driving out of small farmers and the disruption of national food supply systems (Clutterbuck and Lang, 1982; Dinham and Hines 1982; Rama, 1985). Simultaneously both a condition for and an important consequence of these developments is the merging of chemical and food industries as in the case of Unilever (Leopold, 1985; Sorj and Wilkinson, 1985).

Additives, contaminants and convenience food

The increasing entanglement of the food and chemical industries has resulted in the invention and application of numerous additives and contaminants. These tiny materials opened up yet other possibilities, besides canning and freezing, of preserving foodstuffs for many weeks as if they were fresh (Millstone, 1986). Flavours no longer had to be derived from original products, for instance sugar and salt, but could be created completely synthetically. These new technologies, in an important way, furthered the development towards the production of 'convenience foods' and 'fast foods'. A far-reaching consequence, in turn, was the rise of an internationally-oriented fast-food industry with ramifications at the level of distribution, resulting in chains of supermarkets as well as of snack and fast food restaurants.

The proliferation of bio-industry

In traditional agriculture, stock-breeding had been more or less subordinated to the growing of basic vegetable products. With the change in Western consumption from vegetable to animal foods, the raising and holding of stock became subordinated to industry, which led to battery-hens and box-calves (Gold, 1983). The emergence of biotechnology in the 1980s had even more far-reaching consequences. It was connected, among other things, with the shift in the food industry away from production of primary ingredients, such as flour, milk and sugar, to 'the fractioning of these ingredients into their constituent nutrients, carbohydrates, fats and proteins' (Sorj and Wilkinson, 1985: 310; Vergopoulos, 1985: 294; see also the anonymous article in *Food Technology* 1991 on ingredients for snacks). Basic to the extension of the range of applicability of biotechnology in the food industry is the capacity to control the catalytic processes of micro-organisms such as bacteria and enzymes and to reprogramme their genetic properties. Raw materials are reduced to biomass and become interchangeable, while proteins can even be produced from petroleum and natural gas. An important possible consequence of these technologies is the future replacement, in part, of agriculture by industry (Ruivenkamp, 1987).

IMPLICATIONS FOR CONTEMPORARY CONSUMERS AND CONSUMPTION

Trends towards individualisation, characteristic of modern societies, are furthered by a proliferation of fast-food facilities. This development takes place on two fronts: eating at home and eating outside. The time needed for food preparation at home has been drastically reduced with the availability of a variety of prefabricated foods in every supermarket. This is even more the case when kitchens are equipped with advanced equipment and implements like food-processors, freezers and microwave ovens, which follow the tin-opener and the refrigerator. Individual household members can now, quickly and easily, take care of themselves at times to suit their own convenience, which creates greater possibilities for fewer meals being consumed together – although whether this is *actually* the result, in our view, needs further research and documentation.

Choices in eating out are also multifarious: snack-corners and fast-food restaurants of every kind from fish-and-chips and hamburgers to pizzas and kebabs. Suppliers of food, dishes and complete meals are to be found in every street. Not only households and individual consumers, but also industrial, school and sports-centre canteens, as well as hospitals and other institutions of care, are nowadays largely dependent on the convenience products of a sophisticated food industry.

There are consequences other than pleasure and convenience in this preparation and consumption of enormous quantities of food, made possible by advanced technological control over nature. Modern consumers struggle with many fears concerning food. First, they are afraid to eat too much, afraid of abundance and of becoming obese. This problem of quantity sometimes goes together with problems of quality: there is a considerable fear among the consuming public about additives and other strange and suspicious elements in the food (Farrer, 1983; Kapferer, 1985; Millstone, 1986). Worries about health are accompanied by those about taste. Convenience foods taste worse than others, in the opinion of many critical consumers, and they contribute to ecological problems through high energy use and unnecessary waste (Driver, 1983: 132–46). It is reported that the industrial production of flavours even leads to long-term changes in the perception of the senses of smell and taste (Barlösius, 1989). The growing popularity of vegetarianism, macrobiotics, reform and other 'natural' or whole foods can be interpreted as a reaction of the consuming public to this type of development. Belasco (1989) and other authors studied these movements as countercultural reactions to modern ways of living and eating. The loss of control over the long chains of dependency in the phases of production, distribution and preparation of food show the reverse of plenty and ease: one never knows what one is eating. This unease has been expressed, notably in Britain, in a number of 'food-scares' (about, for example, salmonella in eggs and listeria in soft cheese) which, as already noted above, have caused considerable political stir in recent years. According to one or two scientific authorities such as Richard Lacey (1989, 1991), these fears are far from being without foundation. Dutch nutritionists, though, put these scares into perspective: in their opinion, in the Netherlands the food is safe when it arrives in the kitchen, but possible dangers start with what happens next.

The sociological relevance of these tendencies in modern industrial societies, which are closely interwoven with the growth of food technology, have barely been recognised – as the fairly blatant lack of specifically sociological literature among the work reviewed in this chapter bears witness.

10

The Impact on Food
of Colonialism and Migration

Millennia of travelling overseas, followed by colonialism and wide-spread migration, have brought a two-way exchange of foods: the import of staple products and other food stuffs from the colonised to the colonising countries and vice versa. The most well-known examples are potatoes, maize, sugar-cane and salt. These products travelled around the world and were incorporated in foreign diets, each in its own way. This movement of foodstuffs meant the start of the development of what Jack Goody (1982) has characterised as a 'world cuisine'. In this process several phases can be distinguished.

(1) In the wake of Columbus (but in earlier periods too) European expansion was accompanied by an ever increasing exchange and migra-tion of people and foods. The United States especially, but Canada and Australia too, became countries inhabited by populations drawn from many different cultures with a corresponding diversity of eating habits brought from their home countries.

(2) With the industrial revolution came increased opportunities for colonialism and empire-building and possibilities for the exchange of people and foods were enormously enhanced.

(3) After the Second World War the colonial empires gradually crumbled away. This did not, however, bring to an end the processes of migration. On the contrary, new waves of immigrants constantly came back to the 'mother countries' bringing their cuisines with them. Migrant workers from Mediterranean and North African countries moved into Northern Europe and established their own cuisines there. The melting pot of races, cultures and flavours, which has been furthered by mass tourism, is increasingly reflected in the eating habits of peoples from all over the world.

The relevance of these processes of colonisation, de-colonisation and migration for the sociology of eating habits is only sparsely recognised, although historians, anthropologists and ethnologists have paid them some attention.

TRAVELLING FOODSTUFFS AND EARLY COLONIAL
EATING HABITS

The wanderings of foodstuffs like potatoes, sugar-cane and maize have been extensively studied by historians and anthropologists (Salaman, 1949; Braudel 1979, Vol. I; Davidson, 1983; Mintz, 1985). Sidney Mintz traces the introduction and the growing importance of the production and consumption of sugar and the implications for the increasing interdependencies between the Old and the New Worlds. This last theme is elaborated upon by Pelto and Pelto (1983) in their article on the effects of delocalisation of the food supply, in which the local population derives an increasingly large amount of food from distant places through commercial channels. This process of delocalisation is a long-term concomitant of the migration of foods. In industrialised countries, delocalisation has meant a greater diversity of diet; the first beneficiaries were the elite, while more recently other classes have come to benefit from the change. In developing nations, delocalisation has resulted in a poorer diet for all but the wealthiest. The authors considered the Columbian exchange of food and production systems between the Old and New Worlds, the rise of commercial food distribution networks (made possible by canning and other processes discussed earlier), and geographical mobility.

Some historical material is available on colonial food supply and eating habits in the United States and Australia (Farrer, 1980; Hilliard, 1969, 1972). Foods, cooking equipment and food preparation in Colonial America have been studied by Doudiet (1976) and Bennion (1976). The roots of the distinctive Pennsylvania-Dutch cuisine (a misnomer, presumably a corruption – its roots are German: Pennsylvania-*Deutsch*) are traced by studying several editions of *Die Geschickte Hausfrau*, which is considered to be the first ethnic cookbook in the United States (Woys Weaver, 1977). The standard of living and the change in diet at the end of the colonial period is described by Alfredo Castillero-Calvo (1987). While the standard diet in Europe became increasingly vegetarian with the advent of many cereal crops brought from the New World, the same seems to have been true in America with the introduction of European cereals. However, because of the great variety of crops and climates in the New World, not all areas increased their consumption of vegetables at the expense of meat. F. Dawell and other contributors to a special issue of the *Revue Française d'Etudes Américaines* on 'La cuisine Américaine'(1986) present studies of American cookery from various angles.

INDUSTRIALISATION AND EMPIRE-BUILDING

Industrial inventions in the nineteenth century, such as canning and, later, freezing, greatly improved the diet of ships' crews, soldiers and settlers, and contributed to their survival. Salted and dried pieces of meat were replaced by tinned ones which were less vulnerable to decay. It was even possible to import familiar foods, especially vegetables and dairy products from the homelands, into the colonies to supply the white colonial elite. Later on these preserved foods became available to a wider public, in tropical regions too (Den Hartog, 1986). New energy sources and transport facilities were among the factors which made colonial expansion easier; by 1900 it seemed as if the whole world was divided up into Europe and its possessions overseas. Ever more intensive exchanges of people and foods were taking place: not only did a growing number of people of white and mixed colour come to live in the colonies, it also happened the other way around: in the big cities of the colonising countries, for instance London and Paris, communities of native colonial origin sprang up, which maintained many of their original habits, especially their foodways, if at all possible.

The confrontation of established inhabitants by new immigrant groups and their eating habits (in Western countries) and inspection of native foodways by the medical service of the colonial government (especially in tropical areas) have evoked more or less similar responses. These came down to large-scale attempts at change and what was seen as improvement of the diet of the powerless outsider groups. Harvey Levenstein (1985) described such endeavours in the United States around 1900, concerning the recently arrived wave of Italian migrants. Upper- and middle-class philanthropists and reformers tried to improve the appalling living conditions of the new Americans by teaching them how to spend their money. Because food in Italy traditionally involved heavy expenditure as a proportion of the household budget, and also because established Americans had strong prejudices against Italian food, they tried to change Italian eating habits, but without success. Similar attempts were made, and for similar reasons, in the Netherlands just after the Second World War, relating to Indonesian 'repatriants' (Van Otterloo, 1987). In both cases, a few decades later the dishes of these minorities had become very popular among the dominant population.

Another type of response took place during the inter-war years, initiated by medical and nutritional specialists: the establishment of organisations and programmes to improve the food and health conditions of native peoples (Douglas and Khare, 1979, 1984a: 1–39; see also Pelto and Pelto, 1983). In this same context, Marilyn Little (1991) writes on Tanganyika and the lack of success of international organisations. She pleads for an acknowledgement for the groundbreaking work the League of Nations sponsored in the 1920s and 1930s in the then new science of nutrition, which resulted in, among other things, the first internationally recognised table of dietary standards. The information collected through the League's research was applied primarily to improving the health of industrial workers in European nations. However, member nations such as Great Britain were required to conduct nutrition surveys in their overseas territories. British administrative policies in Africa were a key factor in precipitating the shortages for at least one ethnic group, the Sukuma of north-west Tanganyika. The Sukuma were unable to maintain their precolonial subsistence system under the pressure of colonial taxation. The gradual degeneration of subsistence production altered the quality of the Sukuma diet. Colonial medical officers assumed that these crisis diets were the 'traditional' African diets. This assumption, combined with the general racist attitudes of the period, precluded the application of the League's research to African populations under British administration.

Other influences of the colonial situation on native diet were manifold. The same modernising influences on food practices that in an earlier period were felt in the West have in part affected developing countries too: urbanisation, female participation in the labour force and increasing availability of processed foods, especially condensed milk and powdered milk. The powdered milk used for babies has had a revolutionary effect on breast feeding practices. A great deal of comparative research has been carried out, largely from a version of a medical sociological point of view, on this subject and, more generally, on mother-and-child and family food habits in ex-colonial or semi-colonial countries from all over the world. Many examples on Africa, Asia and the Caribbean are to be found in *Social Science and Medicine* (King and Ashworth, 1987).

THE RISE OF IMMIGRANT CUISINES

Colonisation and its aftermath caused people to move to and from both sides of the oceans taking their preferences for food with them and in this way making their own contribution to the diffusion of cuisines. Migrant groups still establish their own little shops and restaurants so that they can continue to eat their own food. This development has been particularly evident since the end of the Second World War.

The phenomenon of immigrant cuisines is fairly well documented in the social sciences (see, for an overview, Calvo, 1982). A general and striking conclusion from this type of research is that immigrants and ethnic minorities try to maintain their own cooking and eating habits as long as possible, even against strong pressures to change them, as we have already seen (Levenstein, 1985). Calvo (1982) analyses eating habits as part of the insertion process of ethnic and cultural migrant groups in a new society. He describes the different activities connected with feeding – expenditure on food, choice of ingredients, substitutions and preparation techniques – and discusses the role of meals for family and cultural identity. An overview of studies of immigrant groups, especially in Europe, attempts to define the relationship between eating habits and major categories of socio-economic position and to identify common factors among the groups studied. A classification of eating styles according to social status is proposed and conceptual tools for this type of analysis are suggested.

Theodoratus (1977, 1983) discusses the continuity and change in eating habits of Greek immigrants to the United States by making a cookbook inventory of typical Greek foods, dishes and spices such as olive oil, garlic, lamb, offal and seafood, and comparing them with their contemporary use by a group of Greek-Americans. The use of garlic for instance has been maintained, although at strategic times such as weekends or in combination with chlorophyll pills so as to diminish the odoriferous impact on other people; the use of Greek (Turkish) coffee is gradually diminishing because it is too troublesome to make and serve to American guests. Freedman and Grivetti (1984) compare types of pregnancy diet in three generations of Greek-American women; first-generation women ate less bread and cereals during pregnancy to ensure a lower birth-weight for the baby, while more women of the second and third generation increased consumption of these products in the belief they would ensure good health. There was a strong tendency among third generation Greek-American women to abandon traditional dietary practices and to adopt 'American' foods.

Besides the eating habits of Greek and Italian immigrants, those of newly established immigrant groups from Asia have been studied too, for instance Chinese families in London and their eating habits (Wheeler and Tan, 1983). Nutritional comparisons have been made between the diets of different ethnic groups, for instance by Harris et al. (1988) who tried to find differences in consumption according to sex, age and ethnicity. The ethnic factor appeared the strongest explanation for the differences found between groups of Anglo-American, Hispanic and Indian background. More of this very specific type of research is noted by Calvo (1982).

Pierre van den Berghe (1984) shares Calvo's opinion of the important relationship between food and ethnic identity. He stresses the ethnic significance of cuisine and explores the persistance of ethnic cuisines in contemporary modern and urban societies. In this type of society, food sharing is a major mark of ethnicity. At the same time, the commercialisation of ethnic cuisine makes its authenticity problematic. He contends that ethnic cuisine is the form of ethnicity whose boundaries are most easily crossed.

In addition to the topic of ethnic food as a continuing means of identity for immigrant outsider groups, the different types of responses to ethnic food by the established inhabitants of Western countries and their development through time, is a most interesting sociological theme. It is, however, much less elaborated on than are the primarily descriptive studies on the adaptation of immigrant groups in foreign countries. Driver (1982) notes the existence of a plethora of different ethnic shops and restaurants, in world cities such as London, as a consequence of the presence of so many ethnic minorities. Some types of ethnic cuisines (for example Italian or Greek) have become popular and even fashionable among settled Londoners. Van Otterloo (1987) traces the long-term development of ethnic cuisines in the Netherlands. She estimates the implications for the mutual relationships between majority and minority groups of their having finally tasted each other's food with approval. Perhaps the table can demolish barriers between people.

The existence of a world cuisine has become a reality. The development towards the internationalisation of eating habits and cuisines has been strongly facilitated by the growth of international food industries and large-scale trade in food (Goody, 1982). Food in Western countries (and also in developing countries for the elites) is available from all over the world, which has far-reaching consequences alike for the composition of diet and for the complexity of dependencies between people for their food. Local variations, however, continue to play an important role. The sociological significance of the aftermath of the age of colonialism being made manifest at the table deserves more attention than it has so far received.

11

The Public Sphere: Professional Cooks and Eating outside the Home

In a general way, sociologists and anthropologists have been aware of the significance of hospitality for sociological theory at least since Marcel Mauss's *Le Don* (1923). Sociological studies of hospitality as an institution in modern societies have not, however, been numerous. The social historian Felicity Heal has recently published an important study (1990) of hospitality in England between 1400 and 1700, but the sociologically crucial differentiation between private hospitality and the commercial restaurants and hotels now often known collectively as 'the hospitality industry' (and of key importance in the national economies of many countries, both industrialised and Third World) came about rather more recently.

It is popularly believed that the restaurant as a social institution dates, in the Western world, only from the French Revolution. The story goes that the skilled professional cooks hitherto employed in the kitchens of aristocrats who had fled abroad or perished in the Terror, finding themselves without work, were obliged to open restaurants and cook for whoever was able to pay and chose to enter. There is a grain, but only a grain, of truth in that. The wide range of modern eating places has quite a variety of institutional precursors besides the post-Revolutionary restaurants. There was certainly nothing new in being able to purchase professionally cooked food and eat it outside the home, at least in the towns. In the cities of medieval Europe, as indeed throughout the world today, 'street foods' (Tinker, 1987) existed in great variety. The cookshop was particularly important to the lower ranks of citizens, for only the larger houses had adequate means of cooking (again, as in many parts of the world today); one could send a joint of meat or pie to be cooked in the baker's oven, or, from cookshops or other vendors, buy a hot dish ready cooked – pies, puddings, meat off the spit, to be eaten at the cookshop or taken home. So there is nothing absolutely new about takeaway and fast foods. Even the popular fish and chip shops of Britain (Priestland, 1972; Reiter, 1991) and Australia antedated the spread of McDonald's by the best part of a century.

The inn too, throughout Europe, for centuries fulfilled a specific social function, of providing meals for the travellers who stayed in them. But at an inn, broadly speaking, one ate what one was given, when one was given it – as Erasmus (*c.* 1518: 64–5) described in his famous account of a German inn. By the eighteenth century, some London inns had a good reputation for a daily 'ordinary', or *table d'hôte* dinner, but they were not places of fashionable resort. As popular meeting places, from the seventeenth century there were in most of the important cities of Europe (Ball, 1991) the coffee-houses or cafés, the outcome of processes both of institutional and product differentiation. Their emergence was also a significant manifestation of the social development of the public sphere (Habermas, 1962), since they served as centres of political intrigue and commercial intelligence. Other lines of institutional development led to the 'private hotel' of early nineteenth-century England (or 'boarding house' in American parlance – Pillsbury, 1990) where residents could order meals either in their own rooms or in a dining room, but were not open to non-residents in the fashion of the great hotels which developed internationally towards the end of that century. Finally, one should not forget such institutions as the works canteen, which emerged in response to the rise of large-scale factory employment and came to be seen as one small element in the development of the welfare state (Curtis-Bennett, 1949); nor the university cafeteria (Grignon, 1986), which traces its ancestry from the monastic refectory.

Closest approximations to the later restaurants, however, both in their social functions and in the food they served, were the taverns of eighteenth-century England. Confusingly, the word 'tavern' was used in colonial America to mean the same as an 'inn' in England (Pillsbury, 1990), but in England 'tavern' originally signified a place where men went to drink wine, as opposed to an ale-house where beer was sold (Mennell, 1985: 137). A tavern was thus from the beginning likely to cater for a socially superior clientèle. By the mid-eighteenth century, many taverns in London were noted eating places and social centres, some large enough to cater for vast municipal banquets, and patronised by the aristocracy and gentry as well as merchants and intellectuals. Contrary to the later pattern, eating out was better established among the English upper classes than among the French. This too was probably related to political patterns: the annual meeting of Parliament in the winter and spring of each year was associated from the seventeenth century with the annual migration of the leading families from their country homes to London for the 'Season' and, apart from the grandest who had their own large London houses, many would stay in lodgings and often 'eat out'. There was no exact counterpart to this in France until after the Revolution, and Mennell has noted (1985: 141) that in the eyes of French noblemen 'to resort to the use of taverns for entertaining in *bonne compagnie* could be seen as analogous to involvement in trade, carrying in milder form the perils of derogation'.

All the same, the first restaurants did begin to appear in Paris *before* the Revolution. The highly restrictive monopoly of the Paris guild of *traiteurs* was breached, and several subsequently famous restaurants opened their doors in the 1780s – which suggests that a market for eating out was developing in elite circles in France as well as in England. It is true, nevertheless, that it was under the Directory and the Empire that the great restaurants of Paris – Beauvilliers, Meot, Les Trois frères provençaux and others – began to set an international model. Competition among them fostered innovation, above all new dishes and an increasingly *haute*, labour intensive and therefore expensive, *cuisine* with 'artistic' pretensions both visual and gustatory. But, from a sociological point of view, at least as significant in the process of competition was the formation of a well-informed and knowledgeable eating *public*. The coffee-houses, taverns and restaurants played a part in making possible a relatively autonomous domain of critical and political public opinion; but restaurateurs were now confronted with a public opinion of their own. The cook's patrons were now many, not few. At first, when it was common for the diner to discuss his (it was a male preserve) dinner with the proprietor and order it a day in advance, the power ratio in the face-to-face relationship of restaurateur and client may superficially have seemed not greatly different from that in the equally face-to-face relationship of the head of a great *ancien régime* household and his master-cook. But the relationship was by now a market relationship, and marked a stage en route towards still more impersonal market-like relations between cooks and consumers with the industrialisation of the food industry in the next century.

GASTRONOMES AND GASTRONOMY

The market was fostered and enlarged by what, rather than the restaurant per se, was arguably the decisive French contribution to eating as a social activity – the invention of the social role of the gastronome (Mennell, 1985: 266–90; Ory, 1986; Pitte, 1991). From Grimod de la Reynière's *Almanach des Gourmands* in 1803 (Bonnet, 1986) and

Brillat-Savarin in the early nineteenth century, through people like
Curnonsky who celebrated French country cooking as an adjunct to
the promotion of tourism after the First World War, there has been a
continuous line of development to the restaurant guides and journalism
of the present day.

'A gastronome', writes Mennell:

> ... is generally understood to be a person who not only cultivates his own refined taste
> for the pleasures of the table, but also, by *writing* about it, helps to cultivate other
> people's too. The gastronome is more than a gourmet – he is also a theorist and
> propagandist about culinary taste. (1985: 267)

Although gastronomy has generally been seen as the preserve of an
elite, laying down canons of 'correct' taste for those wealthy enough
to indulge them, according to Mennell they have also – wittingly or
no – performed a democratising function in the shaping of taste, since
the publication of their writings disseminates elite standards well outside
the most exclusive circles. Mennell argues that the gastronome is an
essentially urban role, associated in the first instance with people
from just below the very highest social ranks, and one particularly
characteristic of periods of social flux. But gastronomy as literary genre
has shown a capacity to survive by changing its emphases and functions
according to changing social circumstances.

Eating out as a form of social activity has a sociological critic in
Joanne Finkelstein (1985, 1989). She views dining out 'as a means
by which personal desires find their shape and satisfaction through
the prescribed forms of social conduct' and thus as an example of
'how human emotions become commodified' (1989: 4). Even a family
visit to McDonald's is promoted as offering the experience of 'a sense
of occasion', while at more exclusive venues, 'pleasure may accrue
from the diner's use of the event to suggest the personal possession
of culturally valued characteristics such as wealth, fine taste and *savoir
faire*'. Choice of a restaurant and choice of what one eats there
are commonly seen as expressions of an individual's own particular
tastes, yet, argues Finkelstein, 'the styles of interaction encouraged
in the restaurant produce an uncivilised sociality. ... The artifice of
the restaurant makes ... us ... act in imitation of others, in response
to fashions, out of habit, without need for thought and self-scrutiny'
(1989: 5). If this is true – and it represents the continuation of a long
line of social theorists' thinking about the 'inauthentic' experience of
self in modern society from Simmel through Marcuse to Baudrillard –
then it is not uniquely true only of dining out. But this line of thought has

always been contested by other sociologists, and it is beyond the scope of this report to explore theories of self which (rather than restaurants per se) are Finkelstein's central concern.

COOKING AND WAITING PROFESSIONS

The restaurant as a social scene has enjoyed a certain intermittent vogue among sociologists, but they have studied mainly interaction among staff, and on the whole paid more attention to waiters than to cooks and cooking. As early as 1920, Frances Donovan published a study of waitresses, but much more famous are Erving Goffman's (1971: 109–40; orig. 1959) memorable observations on waiters moving between the back (kitchen) and front (dining) regions, drawing on that much-quoted sociological source, George Orwell's *Down and Out in Paris and London* (1974 [orig. 1933]). Mars and Nicod's study of *The World of Waiters* (1984), strongly influenced by Mary Douglas, is also much concerned with boundaries and their signification. Another participant observation study of waiters is by Hutter (1970).

William Foote Whyte's studies (1946, 1948, 1949) of the American restaurant industry pointed to a typical pattern of friction arising between waiters and cooks. In most organisations, orders flow down the status hierarchy, but in the case of restaurants this is contradicted by the fact that it is the relatively low status waiters who deal with the customers and then transmit them to the relatively higher status cooks, and demand prompt action from them. This often generates resentment and even a slowing down on the part of cooks, which in turn increases the pressure on the waiters from the paying public. Whyte recommended that friction be reduced by minimising interaction and symbolically increasing the distance between the two groups through the use of relatively impersonal means of placing orders – the written order form, placed on a revolving spindle, or the use of the house phone or a loudspeaker link to the kitchen. Gordon Marshall (1986) studied a large popular restaurant in Scotland which had, by chance, adopted just such measures as Whyte advocated. He noted, as has often been observed in the restaurant industry, that work satisfaction and morale were high, despite not very high pay, and long hours of work often under demanding conditions. He attributed this in part to the 'informal workplace economy' (i.e. fiddles) from which they benefited, and the related entrepreneurial strategy of tolerance and paternalism adopted by the employer towards the staff. But it was also, Marshall argued, due to the 'physical proximity of employee and client, hence physical proximity of work and leisure' in the bar or restaurant. 'The workplace culture of the licensed restaurant embraces the shared belief that bar work, though clearly not a leisure pursuit, is nevertheless different from "real work" such as is undertaken elsewhere, for example in industry' (1986: 33).

There is a general impression that cooks especially derive considerable satisfaction from their work, yet they have attracted relatively little detailed attention from the sociologists of occupations. One reason for the neglect may be that the one name covers so many realities (some of which are made apparent in Schroedl's [1972] graduate student piece of participant observation). As Gary Alan Fine writes, 'cooking is highly internally differentiated, stretching from the lower depths of manual labour to the upper reaches of fine art' (1987: 141). Fine has studied particularly cooks working in the upper part of the range of restaurants, and describes the aesthetic satisfaction and pride they often feel.

> Although cooking is an industrial occupation, part of the 'hospitality industry', it is also intimately connected with aesthetic evaluation. Food must not merely be edible and nutritious, but also look, smell, taste and feel 'good'. This poses particular challenges for cooks, who must be not only labourers, but also 'artists'. ... Yet, unlike the image of artists who specialise in the fine arts, these workers do not have control of their own time, their equipment, and their product. Craftsmen might be a better analogy for what these cooks are. (Fine, 1987: 151–2)

The aesthetic sense and pride are acquired: usually, a new recruit first entering trade school will not have any such sense, but it is acquired during training and on the job. Fine's study of trainee cooks in a Trade School (1985; see also Fine, forthcoming) demonstrates how this takes place. Fine's observations are consonant with Mennell's (1985: 168–99) historical study of associations and journals among chefs at the top end of the restaurant trade in France and England in the late nineteenth and early twentieth centuries. At that time, cooks learned their skills through traditional apprenticeship in the kitchen, often working under terrible conditions for low pay. Yet, especially for the French, the feeling that they were artists, with an aesthetic sensibility, was central to their occupational identity:

> ... however miserable the pay and conditions of the majority, the cooks, although they seem to have had a clear sense of their identity as an occupational group, showed little taste for confrontation with the employers or willingness to take industrial action. The peculiarity of [their] emphasis on the need for progress, improvement, achievement in cookery as such was that this was seen as a *collective* enterprise, something that would be achieved by collaboration among cooks proud of their art. And the result would be not individual mobility but 'stratum mobility' – the

profession as a whole rising within the prestige ranking of occupations generally in society. (1985: 169)

Petersen and Birg (1988) have documented the persistence of artistry and creativity in the occupational self-conception of top chefs. As for Fine's trainees, the aesthetic sense they acquire may be only a vestige of that spirit, but that it survives at all in the trade schools is interesting.

Overall, however, the very diversity of the cooking profession makes it hard to generalise about trends. Paterson's (1981) ethnography of the tedium and drudgery of the work of kitchen maids in a Scottish hospital reveals the 'good' organisational reasons for the unhygenic practices observed. Maids rarely if ever saw meal production through to the finished article – and rarely if ever elected to taste it themselves, opting instead for sandwiches or toast. Theirs was the typical alienation of a worker on an industrial production line. In a study of cooks in Britain, Chivers (1973) spoke of 'the proletarianisation of a service worker', and in the age of the microwave oven when something like three-quarters of eating places in Britain operate principally by reheating industrially prepared products, it is hard not to see deskilling as one component of the total picture. On the other hand, it is also easy to take the image of the great French chefs of the past as typical of the whole profession, whereas a large proportion of cooks were never anything approaching great culinary artists but rather humble kitchen-hands.

Between, on the one hand, government statistics and broad studies of the hospitality industry as a whole (e.g. Medlik, 1972) and, on the other, case studies of a few working kitchens, we lack the detailed sociological research that would make possible better understanding of trends in the very diverse occupation of professional cook. That understanding probably depends also on more detailed studies of regional and national variations in the propensity to eat out, and of the great variety of uses people make of eating out. Studies of the geographical location of eating places (e.g. Smith, 1985; Pillsbury, 1990) may help to plug one gap in our knowledge.

12

Domestic Cookery, Home Economics and Girls' Education

Cooking at home, in contrast with the professional cookery which developed first at the princely courts and subsequently in the newly established restaurants for a bourgeois public, has always been women's business (Mennell 1985: 134ff, 201 ff). As an assumption governing the organisation of the typical household, this association of women and domestic cookery has only recently come under widespread challenge, and we shall review the mass of sociological research on the domestic division of labour in the next section. The present section deals with domestic cookery as such.

Domestic cookery in Western countries underwent a profound change after 1800. From then onwards modernisation and industrialisation had a steadily growing impact on the daily life of ordinary people. Within living memory mothers taught their daughters how to cook and prepare meals according to an oral tradition, in the cities as well as in the countryside. For most of history cookery books were within the reach only of a small literate elite group. With the expansion of schooling and literacy, cookery books multiplied in type and in number until the present day when they are published in torrents. Apart from the rising level of education of the common people, many technical changes in housing and kitchen equipment (like piped water, sewerage, mains gas and electricity) contributed to the development of a more varied and refined style of cooking at home (Schwarz-Cowan, 1985; Strasser, 1982; Van Otterloo, 1990). The remarkable improvement in the general standard of living of the industrialised world since the nineteenth century and especially after the Second World War was another important factor.

National and regional differences in domestic ways of cooking have always played a role, as have divisions of class and religion. Ecological circumstances on the one hand, and the social processes leading to the emergence of nation-states and national identities on the other, are among the primary influences which account for regionally flavoured country cookery. Although ingredients differed a good deal (for instance, olive oil around the Mediterranean versus butter in north-west Europe), the composition of dishes prepared in farmers' households all over Europe were for centuries more or less the same: soups and stews, cooked in one pot over an open fire. In the cities meals did not differ very much from those in the countryside, save for the greater availability of luxurious and more varied ingredients. Class differences were always important though. Bourgeois cookery, derived in part over a long period from courtly models of cooking, reached its culmination in the nineteenth century (Mennell, 1985: 200–29; Teuteberg and Wiegelmann, 1972: 33–45).

COOKERY CLASSES AND SCHOOLS OF HOME ECONOMICS

One of the kinds of knowledge that has been very important in promoting greater uniformity through processes of modernisation and democratisation of cookery styles is nutritional science. Medical knowledge and folk medicine have influenced diet at least since the Middle Ages, but with the diffusion of modern medical and nutritional insights these were quickly viewed as old-fashioned. The new type of nutritional knowledge was to an important extent mediated by bourgeois ladies teaching in cookery classes and writing cookery books. Their pupils were daughters of well-to-do families and lower-class girls who received their lessons in strict separation, according to the principles of the age. At the end of the nineteenth century, schools of home economics and domestic science were established in Europe and America (Mennell, 1985; Russell, 1984; Levenstein, 1988: 72; Van Otterloo, 1990). In these schools the importance of economy, health, hygiene and other bourgeois virtues were heavily stressed. The type of learning can be reckoned among the manifold efforts at organising virtue by bourgeois reformers, physicians and educators, directed at lower-class groups. Dyhouse (1977) pinpoints two contrasting motives underlying teaching cookery to schoolgirls in Britain. One was to teach 'home-thrift' and the skills of making nourishing and tasty meals to working-class girls to help keep their husbands from straying into the alehouses – for working-class women's ignorance and domestic incompetence were held in some measure responsible for poverty, squalor and poor health. The second motive reflected fears of increasing shortages of domestic servants, and sought to raise the valuation of the domestic arts as means of tempting more girls into service. These motives were also important in the Dutch cookery and home economics classes.

The influence of the cookbooks written by the cookery teachers, advocating rational instead of traditional standards of cooking and composition of meals, lasted for nearly a century. Reprints of these collections of recipes appeared again and again, while actual meals and dishes, especially in the 1950s, were very much like those prescribed by these books. Several generations of girls, wives and mothers, especially in 'the high days of the housewife', must in one way or another have been brought directly or indirectly in touch with the way of cooking and home-management advocated by the schools of cookery and home education. This knowledge is nowadays diffused by women's magazines and other means of mass communication. Advertising by large food companies and retailers also makes an important contribution to the public's awareness of new products and ways of preparation. Nevertheless, a caveat should be entered: the sociology of quite how people (children and men as well as women) learn to cook, and quite what use they make of printed materials in the process, is as yet seriously under-researched (for an older but suggestive study, see McKenzie, 1963).

Since the Second World War other far-reaching and, in a certain sense, contradictory developments in domestic cookery have taken place, which simultaneously made women's tasks in the kitchen easier and more complicated. First, the rise in the standard of living and in the general welfare of the population, together with other improvements in technical and material conditions, has made possible higher demands regarding the quality of ingredients and ways of preparation of dishes eaten at home. In comparison with earlier days, domestic cooks must know a lot more about the composition of meals and techniques of preparation, and be able to follow manifold fashions. This makes the task of cooking for a family a more demanding one. Secondly, and in contrast, the expansion of industrial food production has made available an ever-growing supply of food products which are more or less ready for consumption. The recent spread of fast foods and convenience foods may to some extent change the character of women's and housewives' domestic activities, if not their central position in the choice and preparation of domestic meals. Some commentators – not necessarily sociologists – have claimed that women are being deskilled by the advent of convenience foods, and concern has been voiced that poorer women not only do not cook, turning to ready-made frozen meals and so on, but no longer know how to use non-processed raw ingredients. But if this is true, it is poorly documented. Social tendencies towards individualisation, especially of formerly shared activities such as eating meals together, are strengthened. Thirdly, the tendency towards individualisation notwithstanding, most of the recent studies on domestic cookery concentrate on the division of cookery tasks within household and family, especially between men and women, on mothers' nurturing responsibilities for babies and children, and on their specific role in the choice and preparation of their families' food. This focus of research is more or less in line with the aftermath of the ideology of the nineteenth-century bourgeois cookery ladies, aimed at teaching wives and mothers how to care properly for their families. It also corresponds with social reality, practically wholly in the recent past and partly in the present, in recognising that these tasks fall mainly to women. These points will now be taken up in more detail and are further elaborated in Chapter 13 below.

CONTEMPORARY WOMEN'S ROLE IN THE KITCHEN AND FAMILY

As food is used to create and maintain social relationships, it plays a very important role in the primary groups of family and household in which individuals pass through their life cycle. The consequences of social positions in family and household for the production, distribution, preparation and consumption of food and meals form an important topic of research (Goody, 1982; Douglas, 1984a). This mostly pivots on microstudies which refer to the same time and place instead of dealing with developments in a larger societal context, some of which will be sketched below. The place of women and mothers in matters of eating is considered central; therefore they are the people most frequently questioned in this type of research.

Charles and Kerr (1986a, 1986b, 1988) for instance, have studied several aspects of the family food system in England. One of their topics is the distribution of food within the family, in which they distinguish between servers and providers. The nature of decision-making surrounding food provision and the patterns of food distribution are examined. The sexual divisions and power relations which characterise families are found to have an impact on the choice of food for family consumption and on women's own assumptions concerning the food needs of family members. Portions of meat especially are distributed unequally between family members, among whom men have a privileged position, while children and women occupy second and third places. Variations in the extent of such inequalities apparently have to do with the nature of the work undertaken by the marital partners and their relative control over money. The same authors study the contradictory and problematic relationship of women to food (1986a). Women are expected to deny themselves food in order to remain slim and therefore sexually attractive and, at the same time, they have to feed their partners with healthy and nutritious meals (see Murcott, forthcoming c). They conclude that these problems as to women's body images are products of their structural position in society.

Van Otterloo and Van Ogtrop (1989) come to a similar conclusion in their attempt to assess the differences in beliefs and practices of mothers of primary school-aged children belonging to three different social classes in the Netherlands. It appears that ideas of 'good food' for children, tastes and body images and control are all part of one differentiated complex of feelings and behaviour towards food, which shows a subtle range of variations according to class. Mothers belonging to the higher strata seem to impose stricter rules at table on their children, their husbands and particularly themselves than do mothers from lower strata. In their explanation they combine insights of Pierre Bourdieu (1979) and Norbert Elias (1978/82). Fischler (1986a) studied a partly comparable although less extensive topic: French mothers views on what children should eat. He maintains that mothers' remarks on 'the right diet' for a child are revealing of how food is conceived of in dietetic and symbolic terms. The most important value they are striving for, 'balance', is primarily manifested in the choice of two types of foods: dairy products and green vegetables. Fischler, working in the tradition of Mary Douglas, suggests that 'balance' takes the meaning of a cultural construct reducing anxiety-producing symbolic disorder, or what he calls the contemporary crisis caused by an overwhelming variety in food choices without clear norms to follow.

Pill (1983) elaborated on the topic of mothers' views on food and health for their children also. The idea that cooking and eating are embedded in a household and family which is based on a hierarchical organisation of sex (and age) forms, apart from family health, an important theme in Anne Murcott's collection (1983a) to which Pill's article belongs. Ellis (1983) shows how the fundamental division of labour between men and women as providers of income and servers of food can even have violent consequences, while Murcott argues that the cooked dinner 'symbolises the home, a husband's relation to it, his wife's place in it and their relationship to one another' (1983b:179, also 1982). Wilson (1989) considers the family food system in terms of gender, health beliefs, family preferences and status from the point of view of preventative health. This study brings us back to a good deal of similar types of research on food and health in the framework of the family, done by nutritional anthropologists, mentioned in Chapter 4. Susan Starr Sered (1988) finally, sheds some light on the question of how fundamental the cooking task of women can be in a religious context. Among Jewish women in the Middle East it is seen as a no less than sacred act.

DEMOCRATISATION AND THE INFLUENCE OF ECONOMICS AND DOMESTIC TECHNOLOGY

The increasing affluence and the ongoing technical revolution in the kitchen during the last fifty years in Europe, America and other parts of the world that fall within their cultural spheres, have resulted in a profound change of feelings, attitudes and behaviour towards food (Lesitschnig, 1989). The choice and availability of foodstuffs, dishes and meals have enlarged enormously for most people and especially for housewives with cooking responsibilities. The democratisation of cookery techniques and manners of preparation, in former days exclusive to elite circles, by means of school education and other channels of communication, has confronted ever more wives and mothers with a higher level of demands from their family members. The circumstances of affluence, safety and security of living, now more than ever, favour tendencies towards refinement in preparing the family table. In most cases, at least among some social strata, women, although liberated from heavy manual kitchen work, are now expected to prepare elaborate but healthy meals for their guests and their families, which means a new and more complicated burden. This tendency is to some extent counteracted by the common endeavours of food industry and restaurant business, in effect, to banish domestic cookery tasks completely.

INDUSTRIAL FOOD AND EATING OUT: CONSEQUENCES FOR DOMESTIC COOKERY

The proliferation of modern industrial food production has resulted in an enormous supply of foodstuffs of which a large part is convenience or fast food. The successive developments of canning, freezing and biotechnology (see Chapter 9) have resulted in lightening the housewife's burden of domestic cookery. At the same time they have opened the possibility for the individual members of the household and the family to cook and eat for themselves at points in time of their own choice which are in line with their own daily programmes in eating matters (Van Otterloo, 1990: 266–71). The long-established social trend towards individualisation, which continues to pervade modern eating habits (Fischler, 1979), is further strengthened by the contemporary omnipresence of possibilities of eating outside the home (Finkelstein, 1985, 1989). This can be practically in every sphere of life, be it school, work, sports or other forms of entertainment or travelling. Eating out is possible in every form from a mere snack to a complete meal, all in a variety of forms. It is even feasible to buy prepared dinners outside, but take them back to consume within the home, in this way bypassing the once indispensable domestic cook.

The question whether the domestic cook will be superfluous in the future (a situation completely different from the central position the nineteenth-century cookery teachers wanted her to take) is not easily answered, because of the complexity and partly contradictory conditions on which this outcome will depend. As long as domestic cooks are also mothers of small children and/or are dependent on husbands with low incomes, it remains less than probable.

The same question is asked from another point of view by Herpin (1988): does the dinner remain an institution or is it losing its significance for family life in France? One of the trends revealed by investigation based on questionnaires is the 'disorganisation' or change in the constitution of meals; smaller meals, different meals on weekends and weekdays. For the middle classes the family dinner retains its importance, but this is doubtful for the working classes.

13

Food in the Division of Labour at Home

'Food in the division of labour at home' covers a multitude of activities – provisioning and shopping, storage and preserving, preparation and cooking, serving and clearing away, never mind gardening, borrowing and exchange. Moreoever, these activities can be undertaken one in relation to another in a probably unknown variety of ways. Cookbook recipes prescribe an ordering of tasks for the prepartion of a particular dish, but it is just one of a number of possibilities, ultimately limited only by the Humpty Dumpty law of physics that a broken egg cannot be put together again – time is unilinear. In this part of the report we turn to examine what we know of the social organisation of these activities, the distribution both of the labour involved and of the fruits of those labours, concluding with a section that considers the expression and satisfaction of tastes and preferences in the domestic context and that begins a sociological dissection of the catch-all phrase 'food choice'.

As observed at the beginning of the previous section, there is a pervasive assumption that cooking at home, along with housework generally, is women's work. This assumption is well-founded as a description of actual domestic organisation. It is one that can be detected in all kinds of quarters – in cross-cultural surveys (Murdock and Provost, 1973), in magazines, cookbooks and advertising (Murcott, 1983c), in the provision of state welfare benefits for the disabled (Land, 1977; Finch and Groves, 1983), in accounts of the toy pots and pans provided for little girls (Sharpe, 1976), in studies of newly married couples (Mansfield and Collard, 1988). It is reflected in utopian thinking about domestic architecture – for example early feminist campaigns for 'kitchenless' homes in the US (Hayden, 1978) – as well as the actual design of houses – for example in Adelaide and Cambridgeshire (Lawrence, 1982). Afro-Caribbean women in mid-1980s London regarded it as their responsibility, whether they liked it or not, or indeed, whether they did so in practice (Thorogood, 1986); a view also found among women in Sweden (Ekstrom, 1991). Lower-class men in Seville sought to ensure that the ideal of male dominance survives by avoiding the task as soon as they married (Press, 1979). And though the raw materials were produced and brought into the domestic compound by the joint efforts of men, women and children, the preparation of food was the work of Tallensi women in the 1930s (Fortes and Fortes, 1936). Certainly Tallensi men did do some food preparation but, like Australian husbands in charge of the barbecue today, this was confined to feasts and very special occasions.

Variations in time as well as place do little to disturb the related assumption that, in contrast to higher status cooking for the aristocracy or commercial outlets, women bear responsibility for day-to-day domestic food preparation (Goody, 1982). Effectively, women are cooks whereas men are chefs. It is not that men do not cook at home: they do (Murcott, 1983b) – an important point to which we return below. But they can elect whether to do so where women have no option. Men 'help' (Oakley, 1974b), are 'understudy' cooks (Murcott, 1983d) but 'they do not commonly take over the main meals, however competent they might be in the kitchen' (Collins, 1985: 71).

Though this set of assumptions has long remained in place, what has altered over the last thirty years or so is the manner in which sociologists have examined it. Early work in this period was not explicitly the study of food preparation, housework or even the household, so much as an extension of the study of the family. In Britain, for instance, the empirical studies of Young and Wilmott (Young and Wilmott, 1957; Wilmott and Young, 1960) and later, their book on the symmetrical family (Young and Wilmott, 1975) had become very widely known, and Bott's (1957) attention to styles of marital relationship and the organisation of spouses' activities caught sociologists' imagination. From the US, Parsons' more theoretical emphasis on the nature of the modern family, its place and function not least as a unit of consumption rather than production, found an echo in British work, such as Fletcher's (1962). The early 1960s saw increased effort though only slow development. Following Bott's lead, there was a flurry of 'who does what round the house' studies, seeking, largely unsatisfactorily, to operationalise her insights concerning the segregation or otherwise of conjugal relationships (e.g. Harrell-Bond, 1969; Turner, 1967; Platt, 1969). Noting the considerable increase in the proportion of married women in the labour force since the Second World War, but impinging little on conventional presumptions about domestic work, women's 'two roles' – home and a job – were clearly proclaimed (see in particular Myrdal and Klein, 1968). At the same time, this was still the period when women's, as distinct from men's, employment was automatically cast as a variety of problem (see Brown, 1976).

By the second half of the 1960s, however, changes in focus were just beginning. Gavron (1966) gave sociological voice to the discontents of British (middle-class) women styled as 'just a housewife' and at around the same time what was then called the Women's Liberation Movement was firmly imported to Britain from the US with the publication in Britain of Friedan's *The Feminine Mystique* (1965).

Thereafter, the terms and approach altered significantly. Critical of the earlier work, the emphasis shifted from Young and Wilmott's symmetrical view of sharing and marital democracy. Now, rather more thoroughgoing empirical study suggested their assessment was little more than unwarranted optimism (see for example Edgell, 1980; Leonard, 1980; Tolson, 1977; and also Oakley, 1974b). And this later work improved on earlier studies of the domestic division of labour by going beyond behaviourist enquiry about who does which tasks, to consider the meaning attached to them by marital partners. So, for instance, the distribution of work turned out not to correlate neatly or in terms of equity with participants' judgements of the importance of each task. As Edgell (1980) showed, even middle-class couples, purportedly more democratic than those lower down the scale, thought of kitchen work as both the wife's responsibility and of lesser importance in the family scheme of things.

After the pioneering work of Lopata's *Occupation: Housewife* (1971) and Mainardi's (1980 [orig. 1968]) early 'women's liberation' piece on housework, Oakley finally (1974a, 1974b), at least in Britain, rescued housework from sociological obscurity and sought to analyse domestic work as a 'job like any other', considering housewives' work satisfaction, routines and supervision. While this line of enquiry has undoubtedly illuminated much of women's domestic lives that was conventionally rendered invisible, it has perhaps not gone far enough. The study of food preparation, cleaning, laundry and the work of running a home as an *occupation* needs to attend, in addition, to features such as quality control, timekeeping, client- as well as worker-satisfaction – and perhaps further consideration of who, if anyone, is a housewife's boss. As will be seen later, each of these is implicated in the investigation of home-based eating.

By the mid-1970s, a full-blown contempt had dismissed the Parsonian view of the family as the affective respite (for men) from the stress of the instrumental world beyond the front door. From empirical work such as the comparative mental health of married/single men/women (e.g. Gove and Tudor, 1973), the persistence of gender-linked stereotyping in education, advertising and the media (Sharpe, 1976; Hartnett et al., 1979), the 'rediscovery' of domestic violence (for example Dobash and Dobash, 1980), to reassessment of conceptual frameworks (Stacey, 1981), not only was the private world of family and household coming in for less rosy-eyed scrutiny, but its relation to the public domain was to be reconsidered (e.g. Gamarnikow et al., 1983).

The occupational and industrial aspects of housework provided additional means of examining the relationship of the domestic division of labour to the economic structure as whole (see Middleton, 1974; Finch, 1983). More recent commentary proposed that the view of the family as stripped of all but the residual economic function of consumption is ill-conceived and over-simplified. Domestic labourers are to be thought of as feeding, sustaining and refreshing the existing labour force and playing a key part in reproducing that of the future – as well as providing a reserve of labour themselves. The precise manner in which the political economy – the 'domestic labour debate' – is to be accounted, however, remained the subject of dispute (West, 1980; Fox, 1980; Wajcman, 1981; and, for a somewhat different view, see Valadez and Clignet, 1984).

Food preparation, cooking and kitchen tasks remained buried in these literatures, and continued to be so as sociological work in the area took further turns. Two related trends are discernible, each with obvious antecedents in the previous decades' work. The domestic labour debate appears to have been less prominent through the 1980s. It has been overtaken, at least in Britain, by those empirical studies located at the conjunction of work on labour markets, the 'black' or informal economies spurred by increased attention to the nature and consequences of unemployment (Gershuny and Pahl, 1983; Pahl, 1984; Harris and Morris, 1986; Laite and Halfpenny, 1987; Morris, 1990; Rees, forthcoming). Threaded through this empirical work is a concern with the relative positions of men and women – a second trend in which the vigorous calls for feminist sociology and social anthropology have been inescapable.

Thinking in terms of women's 'two roles' has given way to a much franker recognition of the 'double burden' which women must shoulder. Women continue to bear the responsibility for the preparation of meals, even when they are in paid employment (Hunt, 1980; Pollert, 1981; West, 1982). The intrusion of modern technology into the kitchen provides only partial and equivocal relief from this dual load (see Chapter 12). Conventional wisdom holds that the electrified kitchen relieves drudgery, improves performance and above all saves time. Yet, as the critics of this wisdom point out, the very success of this technology means that standards of proper housewifely performance have also risen dramatically. Any discussion of the impact of technology must be located in pre-existing political, social and economic contexts (Thomas and Zmroczek, 1985). Thus, Bose (1979) has argued that since technology allows a lighter domestic load, women are able to take on new burdens. Lightening the domestic load perpetuates women's capacity for bearing additional paid commitments (Murcott, 1983c).

The 'liberating' potential of 'convenience' foods needs to be analysed in the same vein – though to see this we must first dispel the clouds of moral and political anxieties which surround such foods; anxieties which stem from classic worries about the condition of the modern family and the decline of commensality (treated elsewhere in this volume). These considerations have yet to be fully incorporated into empirical study and theorising about the place of foodstuffs that are increasingly highly processed industrially before entering the home has barely begun (Dare, 1988).

Women's lack of power relative to men within marriage, family and the home itself, is reflected and reinforced by the position of each in the market for wage labour (see Huber and Spitze, 1983; Bryson, 1985). It is thus likely that any aspirations women may have (female, but not male, students in Japan [Koshi, 1988] want a more equitable distribution of both management and labour in the home) will continue to be frustrated. Nonetheless, the increasing sociological acknowledgement of the asymmetry of power between men and women has highlighted the service element in women's share of domestic work. This is nowhere more evident than in the preparation and presentation of food. English usage underscores the point: meals are served, individuals are presented with servings – or, in Australia, with serves. The way women perform this service differs according to their station in life. In a classic study of a Cheviot parish (on the borders of Scotland and England) in the 1940s, the 'tea ceremony' nicely revealed the economic and cultural distinctions of that rural locality; some of which are still clearly evident today. In the middle-class house, the woman's role was enshrined in a graciousness bestowed on others round the table as she offered them their food. In the working-class house, the woman's role at table was more obviously that of waitress (Littlejohn, 1963). Nonetheless, though their styles differed, both served.

As the literature constantly reiterates, the convention dies hard that in wage economies men are the breadwinners and women the homemakers. It is the manner in which the actual labour of food preparation is embedded in domestic power relationships and their relative positions in respect of the means of production of the food to be consumed that constructs women as servers, men as served (Murcott, 1983d; Kerr and Charles, 1986). Women's activities in relation to food and drink, like those in relation to any other sphere of life, are controlled by men (Kerr and Charles, 1986); something that holds true even on those festive occasions that women hold for their female friends, as Honkasalo's ethnography of Finnish women's sauna parties neatly shows (1989).

A 'feminist perspective' has thus focused sociological attention on gendered power relationships in the production, service and consumption of food. It has also the rarely mentioned consequence of rendering those parts of that literature that are not written from an explicitly feminist viewpoint available to be read as if they were. However, while concentration on a feminist viewpoint is crucially important, it also runs risks. One danger is that it limits sociology's credibility. Those (men?) outside the discipline who are impatient with, and probably ignorant of, the nice distinctions concealed by the designation 'feminist', remain sceptical of analyses that appear to them simply to show that women, once again, are unjustly disadvantaged. They claim that the days of wifely servitude are done, drawing on personal experience and anecdote or pointing to market research surveys which report that men (and children) do participate in domestic food activitites. Such unreconstructed attitudes are best and most forcefully met by compelling research evidence – which brings us to another of those risks.

One danger of a purely 'feminist perspective' is that such a viewpoint can too readily eclipse suitably subtle and detailed enquiry into the fine and complex grain of the social organisation of domestic interiors. Interpretations of data which show that women bear a greater share of food work at home than do men, have *also* to attend to questions about the albeit typically smaller share that men do bear. What work do men *routinely* do – as opposed to their being a reserve of labour in emergencies? What explanations can be found for the distributions of effort that are reported? How does this fit with an anlysis of the overall political economy of households? What is the impact of the presence or absence of dependent children? And do we not have to cater for this impact's being dynamic as children grow older during the fifteen and more years they are typically co-resident with their parents/caretakers?

We have only the merest straws in the wind to begin to answer this range of questions. Few studies address those concerning the impact of co-resident dependent children in older age groups. Pahl's (1984) cross-sectional study in South-eastern England reports generally higher levels of men's participation in domestic labour in households that no longer contain dependent children than in those that do. For South

Wales, Barker (1972) reports a parental indulgence that expects little of adult, unmarried sons *and* daughters in the way of either financial or practical contribution to the home. And Zackon's early (1970) and apparently unpublished work contains a single, tantalising case reporting the negotiation between a teenage girl and her parents whereby she is allowed to prepare food of her own choice rather than of her mother's, on condition that she still eats with the rest of the family.

We have as few leads on the question of men's participation in food work. Murcott's study of 1979/80 (1982, 1983b, 1983d) offers suggestive lines of enquiry – though any general conclusions are limited by the small size of the sample and reliance solely on women's reports of the division of domestic labour. Nonetheless, what it suggests is that women can and do derive some pleasure and satisfactior in providing both culturally aceptable meals – centrally, the 'cooked dinner' (Murcott, 1982) – and in catering for individual household members' likes and dislikes (Murcott, 1983d). Doing this also reassures them that in attending to members' needs they are suitably conforming to what is expected of women as wives and mothers. But there are other, more subtle features of the evidence (Murcott, 1983b). One intriguing feature concerns the nuances of meaning enshrined in women's discussions of food work – what did they mean precisely by the verb 'to cook' or the adjective 'cooked'? A second concerns women's own reports that their husbands could, and indeed did, undertake certain food work, fairly routinely. The resulting provisional analysis reveals a distinct set of correspondences. Cooking refers to preparation of a whole meal – commonly a main meal, typically a 'cooked dinner'. Cooking thereby stands in contrast to other types of food preparation – not merely simpler instances, such as snacks or breakfast, but also potentially complex affairs, that may lie outside the core of culturally familiar styles of eating, such as 'curry'. Cooking, in its meaning as main meal preparation, is held to be the responsibility of women, other forms of food preparation more readily the province of men. As Murcott noted at the time, her analysis is highly speculative:

> Its purpose is to indicate future lines of enquiry. Much more systematic and thoroughgoing work needs to be undertaken exploring not only the meaning people attach to cooking and kitchen work but also the relation of those meanings to the social organisation of households and the social relationships involved in a gender linked division of labour. Just possibly, it will turn out that it is not so much that women do the cooking, as what is called cooking is the work that women do. (Murcott, 1983b: 184).

A most welcome contribution to the literature that does pursue this line of enquiry has, however, very recently appeared. DeVault's (1991) book examines the activities involved in feeding the family in the city and suburbs of Chicago during 1982–83. Based largely but not exclusively (she included some male partners) on interviews with women with dependent children, her study also pays close attention to household members' associated interpretative frames of meaning.

Though conscious of having few data, she presents a fine discussion of her evidence concerning the three men in her sample of thirty households who cooked more than occasionally. So, for instance, she notes that in one case, the man routinely undertook core food work, but did so 'under instruction' – his wife organised the routines and took on the burden of reminding him of what needed to be done each day. Or again, DeVault comments on the contrast between the way that when women talked about food work, they took their husbands' and childrens' preferences (see the next two sections below) as fixed points around which they planned the meals, whereas reference to such constraints were mostly absent from the men's reports. So too, she notes that where women would berate themselves for their own faults in food-work, one man's matter-of-fact reporting of his own lapses, 'while perhaps more reasonable, is striking in its lack of shame' (DeVault, 1991: 150).

Until further investigations along such lines are pursued and researchers introduce greater sensitivity to folk usages in commonplace terms with apparently shared meanings, confirming the worth or otherwise of speculation such as Murcott's, remains on the agenda. It probably also means that investigations that persist in casting their question as 'who does the cooking' are very likely to persist in getting the answer 'the women' – thereby persisting in missing the opportunity even to begin to penetrate the complex relation between the attribution of shared meanings and the actual distribution of labour, never mind the place of both in the overall political economy of the household.

INTRA-HOUSEHOLD FOOD ALLOCATION

There is ample evidence historically and cross-culturally of the differential distribution of food according to types of social status that become especially evident *within* households, notably those based on gender, age or both (Des Gupta, 1987; Rizvi, 1991). Pointing to the need for those concerned with the causes of malnutrition to examine distribution patterns within households, Pelto (1984) provides comparative social anthropological illustrations of cultural correspondences between gender/age and food prescriptions/proscriptions. She is careful to note that in some societies a disproportionate share of calories and protein is directed to men, but that elsewhere children or adolescents may be particularly favoured, while in others they are disadvantaged (and see Chapter 7 on Patterns of Food Consumption).

Fragments of historical data point in similar directions. While the poverty studies of the early part of this century obviously included diet, they were not always sensitive to the *intra*household distribution of what food was available. Rowntree, for instance, converted wives' and childrens' consumption to the common basis of the diet provided 'per man per day' (Rowntree, 1901: 229). Between the wars Spring Rice (1939), on the other hand, explained that the tactics adopted among the British urban working class of the 1930s in the face of financial stringency entailed a deliberate redistribution such that the mother would be the first to go without. The children had to be fed, supplemented if necessary by the school, and her husband must be fed, as upon him depends the 'first of all necessities – money' (see also Davies, 1978: 58 [orig. 1915]). By the end of the Second World War, Le Gros Clark was still raising the question. As he told a meeting of the Nutrition Society he was confident that food was by then more equitably distributed *between* households. He was, however, sure that it may yet remain unevenly distributed *within* them – a matter requiring, he believed, anthropological and sociological investigation (Le Gros Clark, 1945).

Nutritionists turning their attention to similar historical fragments have observed that we need to recall the state of contemporary nutritional knowledge. For instance, the nineteenth-century view that made Oliver Twist's request for 'more' so outrageous predates modern scientific understanding that growth requires extra calories. Dickens's contemporaries assumed that because children were smaller than adults, they needed less to eat (Drummond and Wilbraham, 1939). As a result, asking for a second helping could only be seen as sinfully gluttonous.

A social scientific view of historical evidence of differential distribution, however, goes further than just noting the state of scientific nutritional knowledge. For instance, Delphy (1979) has reported that in nineteenth-century rural France, men regularly received larger amounts of food than did women, children or the infirm elderly. They were also accorded the choicest foods; if home-reared poultry appeared on the table, men had the superior cuts, and when butcher's meat became available now and then, it was reserved for the men. This pattern of distribution was rendered invisible by conventions that were supported by such beliefs as 'women eat less than men' and shared precepts that since vegetables do not 'hold to the body' they are insufficient for men (see Chapter 7).

Women's position in a domestic division of labour is, it is argued, intimately linked to the ensuing household distribution of food. It underpinned dietary differences between men, women and children in Pennsylvania in 1910 (Levenstein, 1988: 101) – where wives prided themselves on the elaborate meals made only when men came home for lunch. And Graham uses the same explanation when reviewing British evidence for such dietary patterns among the poorer sections of the British working class of the 1970s and 80s; 'as part of her role as the provider of food, it is the mother's responsibility to ensure that her husband and her children are well fed' (Graham, 1984: 130). Though the data are sparse, the differential access to foods can be argued to reflect men's position vis-a-vis providing for the home as much as it does women's. For instance, Luxton (1980) provides a vivid example of working-class Canadian men's successfully claiming sole use of alcohol brought into the house, on the grounds that earning the money correspondingly earned them such a right to this luxury item.

Against this background, Kurt Lewin's suggestion, in a classic paper in the field (1943), that women serve as 'gatekeepers' controlling the flow of food into and within the household, seemed reasonable for a very long time. But, as McIntosh and Zey (1989) remark, this assumption may not withstand close scrutiny:

> Studies of task distribution and decision-making in the family do show that women make decisions about food purchases and do the actual purchasing, storing and preparing of food, but observers have drawn the unfounded conclusion that women thus control the flow of food into the family. *Responsibility* is not equivalent to *control*. (1989: 318)

Even in advance of the availability of an adequate body of data, there are obvious grounds for pursuing the emerging analytic framework that views the social organisation of domestic interiors as integral to the socio-economic context of which it is part. Clearly poverty is not the sole circumstance under which differential access to food within the home is evident – although in some parts of the world persistent poverty is too readily overlooked in analysing inequitable food distribution (Rizvi, 1991). In any case, achieving abundance in supplies of adequate food creates the circumstances in which the individuated expression of preference can assume considerable prominence (Jerome, 1975). And (as will be seen in the next section) a sociology of choice and taste is pertinent to understanding intrahousehold distributions. The allocation of food needs in any case to be set in the context of the distribution of and access to other household resources. Existing distribution patterns of material goods have yet fully to be investigated. Jan Pahl (1980, 1982, 1989) has made a major contribution in her discussion of financial allocations in marriage. Graham (1984) has reviewed the available work on less well-off British households, showing women's disadvantaged access to transport, housing, fuel and money as well as food, coupled simultaneously with having to bear responsibility for the health and welfare of their men and their children. However, we still know little about intrahousehold allocations of items such as clothing (but see Corrigan, 1989), sports equipment, magazines or whatever – items which hover between those that are obviously domestic and those that are, on the face of it, more personal, but yet are assumed to be made available from within households. Still less do we have a sociology of all this.

The investigation of home based resources has, moreoever, to encompass more than simply attending to material goods. The disposal of time has to be included (Gershuny, 1982). Not only is time itself a resource to which men, women and children enjoy differential access – is there such as thing as women's leisure time? (Deem, 1986). But, as Wallman (1984; see also Berk and Berk, 1979) has imaginatively shown, there are sophisticated trade-offs to be made between the disposal of material resources, especially money, and the use of time either to acquire the means whereby other goods and services can be obtained, or to undertake the labour oneself of providing goods and services considered necessary or desirable.

The distribution of food in the home, as this section has illustrated, is, then, a matter both of quantity and type – though at times it is hard to discern the distinction in the literature. Indeed, for analytic purposes, there is a case for *not* emphasising the distinction. For moving beyond initial description of 'patterns' of distribution demands a grasp of the social organisation of food production and consumption and, once again, the power relationships within which they are embedded.

THE CHOICE OF FOOD AT HOME

If the portrayal of patterns in food consumption and distribution (see Chapter 7) is only the first step on the way to sociological analysis, then 'food choice' is a shorthand that is also pre-sociological. At some general level, use of the word choice conveniently summarises selection from whatever range of foodstuffs people have available to them – as found, for instance, in a single edited collection that includes market researchers' examination of food presentation or changes in 'lifestyle' (King, 1979; Lowe, 1979) and social nutritionists' discussions of both economic trends (McKenzie, 1979) and the relationship between nutritional knowledge and patterns of food consumption (Thomas, 1979). In remaining silent, however, on the mechanisms whereby selection can be exercised, such usages run the risk of eclipsing enquiring into those mechanisms.

The sociological task in studies of choice as a component of consumption, whether of food or anything else, is, at least, threefold: to uncover native understandings, where they exist, of the very expression 'choice'; to identify culturally derived obstacles and opportunities for its exercise; to examine its politico-economic context. Work on food choice in the home has emphasised some of these more than others, and shown that such divisions are always somewhat arbitrary; indeed, for women the term choice is only partly appropriate. Juxtaposing two British studies referred to in earlier parts of this report both illustrates this and summarises many of the points made in the previous two sections.

One study is that of Murcott (1982, 1983b, 1983d, also 1988b, and forthcoming c); the other is that of Charles and Kerr (1986a, 1986b, 1986c, 1987, 1988; Kerr and Charles, 1982, 1986). The first was a study of 40 young women and mothers in the southern part of Wales, conducted along standard ethnographic lines; the second was a sample survey of 200 young mothers in an urban area of northern England which used qualitative data but gathered and analysed them in a rather different fashion from that of Murcott. Despite these important differences in method the evidence from both studies is closely parallel.[7]

The notion of 'proper meals' is central to the findings from both studies. The term refers to the main meal of the day, consisting above all, so it was found, of a course within the meal composed of meat, potatoes and vegetables, with superior variants on Sundays and at Christmas. This notion is the key to understanding the complex set of relationships which food involves for women: relationships to their husbands and children, to themselves, to their own diet, and to their ideas of goodness, health and vitality. Thus, for example, the consumption of proper meals represents and reinforces the division of labour and power differentials within the family. Producing the meals themselves is women's work – part of the familiar family ideology that women are the homemakers while men earn the family wage, an ideology which gains prominence with the arrival of children and women's (possibly temporary) withdrawal from the waged labour

---

[7] Juxtaposing these two studies not only permits illustration of the sociological task to be tackled, it also rehearses the manner in which enquiries adopting different research approaches contrast with but also may complement one another. In a newly developing field of enquiry bedevilled not only by so many unanswered questions, but by questions still to be suitably sociologically formulated, an appreciation of the literature that is so far available has actively to remain alert to the significance of the relative strengths and limitations of the research styles and stances adopted. Behind the present pair of instances, lies the very familiar, but nonetheless vital, observation concerning the relative strengths and limitations of different empirical research approaches, and the trade-offs made in adopting one or another type. In principle, survey research designs, such as that adopted by Charles and Kerr, emphasise hypothesis testing and a deductive analytic attitude, thereby reaping the important benefits of larger numbers, and greater statistical representativeness. Correspondingly, though their interview data were audio-tape recorded – and described as qualitative – Charles and Kerr were nonetheless constrained by the impetus and tenor of a survey design. Thus the analytic strategy they adopted entailed treating their data as 'open ended' answers within a survey; the material was subjected to a content analysis to derive a coding frame according to which it was thereafter 'coded for the computer' (Charles and Kerr, 1988: 7).

This research approach stands in contrast to the ethnographic attitude adopted by Murcott. This stance is more dynamic and fluid – allowing the accumulative incorporation of insights gained in any one stage of fieldwork into subsequent stages – and also more deliberately and self-consciously emphasises an inductive attitude to data analysis. Ethnographies are not intended to be statistically representative and being single-handed means that only relatively small numbers of informants, cases or settings can be accommodated in any one study. The strength of ethnography, however, is a central preoccupation with the excavation of nuances of meaning and interpretative frameworks.

market. Being charged with the provision of a kitchen service brings a parallel injunction to provide according to the tastes and preferences of the beneficiaries of that service. Women cook for others and privilege the choice of family members, especially husbands', over their own.

This complex assembly of roles, powers and duties took precise cultural and culinary forms. Thus, in her study of the recurrent native expression, 'cooked dinner' (aka 'meat and two veg') Murcott (1982) showed that informants could, with ease, present clear 'rules' for its composition, preparation, presentation, timing and the proper occasion for its provision. Women's accounts of the place of this meal in domestic life demonstrated both its significance in symbolising the home, and men's and women's respective roles in – and contributions to – it.

Other intriguing findings emerged from these studies. Like the rural inhabitants of both nineteenth-century France and 1970s south-eastern England (Newby, 1983) Charles and Kerr found that cultural assumptions supported differential food provision; men were believed to need more than, and different types of food (especially meat) from, women. These assumptions were of a piece with women's main role of providing the meals at home that are acceptable to their partners.

Feeding children at the same time as feeding husbands complicates the picture. Women face a complex of contradictory obligations. As homemakers, they are charged with keeping the peace and are required to ensure conflict-free family life. Simultaneously, they are to defer to their husbands' authority, cannot fail to acknowledge his superior power and are obliged to provide food according to his taste. Feeding children gets caught up in loving and pleasing them, expressed in, among other things, acquiescence to their demands for one food rather than another. At the same time, children must be tutored and their good manners in eating – at mealtimes as well as others – ensured. And as if all this was not enough, women are also guardians of the family health, and, as reminded by health advisors from the moment they expect their first child (Graham, 1979) are responsible for infant health and development. Faced with all this, it is small wonder, Charles and Kerr imply, that women often use sweet foods as a treat, pandering to their children and pacifying them when their activities threaten family harmony, even though to do so only fosters anxieties about their healthy growth.

A woman's own individual relationship to food also presents further contradictory choices. Not only is she setting aside her own menu preferences in deference to her husband's tastes, not only does food planning and provisioning take up a very large part of her day, she is also acutely conscious of herself as a female. A slim, attractive body must be striven for and maintained. She knows this is expected through public and media images of desirable femininity. She has found this reinforced in her contact with ante-natal services where weight control is a component of education for health. And she regularly finds the desirability of slimness reinforced by both her husband and her peers. Thus, women's self denial at table can serve the aim of both sexually alluring slimness and the maternal woman's role that puts family first.

The other side, as it were, of those cultural definitions is revealed in the data extract cited below. What is so telling in this discussion of the meaning of cooking is that without prompting or hesitation, the informant couched it in terms of her relationship to her husband, in terms of his tastes and comfort, and with reference to their mutual conjugal obligations:

> I think it lets him know that I am thinking about him – as if he knows that I am expecting him. But it's not as if 'oh I haven't got anything ready' ... Fair play, he's out all day ... he doesn't ask for that much ... you know it's not as if he's been very demanding or – he doesn't come home and say 'oh, we've got chops again', it's really a pleasure to cook for him, because whatever you ... oh I'll give him something and I think well, he'll like this, he'll like that. And he'll always take his plate out ... and he'll wash the dishes without me even asking if I'm busy with the children. Mind, perhaps his method is not mine .... (Murcott, 1983d: 78)

Not only is she honouring her obligations as a good wife to have a meal ready, she takes a pleasure in so doing, and is correspondingly appreciative of her husband's pleasure in his food and of his practical help; which in turn acknowledges that she is suitably honouring her own womanly obligations (see also DeVault, 1991).

In short, putting husbands and children's food choices above their own rests in part, on an acknowledgement of the pleasure of eating (Murcott, forthcoming c) and in part on the pleasure of 'job satisfaction' of catering for the legitimate enjoyment for others. Yet as Charles and Kerr stress, although eating can be a pleasure for everyone, it is a pleasure than many women have great difficulty in allowing for themselves; indeed, eating often induces guilt in the face of the cultural definitions of what a wife should do and what a woman should look like.

This extended account of these two studies provides graphic illustration of the manner in which food choice is inextricable from cultural expectations and the micro-politics of domestic interiors – and in the process casts doubt on the relevance of the word 'choice'. As one of Charles and Kerr's respondents explained:

> Mine [likes and dislikes] tend to get pushed to the background I must admit. The things that I like that nobody else likes I very rarely get. It's usually easier to cook

something that I know they [her husband and children] will eat than what – well I
mean, I wouldn't go out and think 'well I'm having this and I want this'. I tend to
get what the majority like which, ten out of ten, it's not my favourite. (Kerr and
Charles, 1982: 7)

And though located in an industrialised economy, this example's analytic implications are not peculiar to it. Whitehead (1981) illustrates
the case in north-east Ghana where self-reliance on food production
coexists with increasing commoditisation. She shows that women's
conjugal obligations, their responsibility for feeding the children and
their differential location in food subsistence as well as cash crop
production compared to men, has led to an intensification of women's
work. In the process, women have little effective control over either the
amount of staple foods produced or how it is disposed of.

The strength of empirical work such as Whitehead's over Charles
and Kerr's lies in the fact that the social anthropological attitude is
better attuned to uncovering mechanisms such as those affording and
constraining the exercise of choice. Although she does not give details,
it can reasonably safely be assumed that Whitehead not only held
conversations with (interviewed) women, but also talked to men and
children. Moreover, it is as likely she was able to observe at least some
relevant activities, events and interactions as they occurred. Charles and
Kerr had to rely on a pair of specially arranged interviews, supplemented
by women keeping a diary record over two weeks. Moreover, like
Murcott's study, their work is hampered in confining its attention to
women. As Murcott noted later:

... to consider women, their work responsibilities and viewpoint alone is but half the
equation. What is also needed is consideration of men's part in the household, and
how they view their own place in it, their view of women's place in it and their
account of the interior of home-based life and activities. (Murcott, 1986: 90–1)

Some consideration of the part played in home-based food production
and consumption by children and any other co-resident household member must also be included in this much fuller approach to the household
economy.   This way, the benefits of insights into substantive differences between spouses' accounts of household life (Berk and Smith,
1980) can be incorporated. This way, brief forays into 'role conflicts'
between housework and child care (Toms Olson, 1979; Backett, 1982)
can be more suitably situated analytically and the ethnocentric confla-
tion of family and household can at last be disposed of (Brannen and
Wilson, 1987). Households will no longer be erroneously assumed to
consist of heterosexual couples and their 'resulting' dependent children,
or the remnants thereof in the 'empty nest' once the young have departed

– or worse, tacitly taken to be the norm from which variants constitu ⸾ deviant instances. The variability of, and changes in, family structures, for example following divorce and remarriage (Burgoyne and Clark, 1983) and consequent altered household formations can be adequately encompassed. And assumptions of either kinship or of heterosexuality in co-residence can, at last, be disposed of (Murcott, 1986).

Many of these thoughts are catered for in the research agenda recently proposed by Sharman and her colleagues (Sharman et al., 1991). Though centrally concerned with diet, they make it quite plain that investigating the production, allocation and choice of food in the home needs to be set in the context of political economy. Moreover, flexibility is required in defining units of study:

> ... women's (and children's and sometimes men's) performance of typically domestic activities is often closely interwoven with a range of other food-acquisition and income-generating tasks, so that the domestic domain is not a clearly discrete and separate one. In addition, in many societies food-related activities (acquisition, distribution, consumption, and associated storage and preparation) and other undertakings that affect the diet, nutrition, and health of domestic units and their members (such as child care, care of the sick, daily maintenance of the living space, and budgeting of cash) are not all carried out by the same group of people. (Sharman et al., 1991: 8)

So the range of domestic groupings need to be identified, along with their internal workings, as an integral part of the investigation of food choice (as much as any other domestic based activity). As Sharman and her colleagues note, there are still very few studies that focus on detailed analysis of the internal dynamics of domestic units in relation to dietary practices. They grant that such studies are time consuming and difficult, but insist that they are of critical importance to an understanding of the acquisition, allocation and use of resources, decision making and the distribution of food.

We have, then, a series of developments in the sociology of the domestic realm and the place of food work within it. Notably, they include the extension of analytic attention to ever finer detail of culturally attributed meaning and interpretative frameworks on the one hand, and to the very definition of the household and to its articulation with the macro social political economy on the other. Such developments provide a promising sphere in which fundamental sociological notions, such as power, autonomy and control (that are inseparably allied to forms of social stratification) are made available for the beginnings of an adequate sociological analysis of the home-based distribution of food and of the apparently individuated expression and satisfaction of food choice.

This part of the report cuts across and overlaps with others. Here we pay special, if brief, attention to food provision and eating in institutions – hospitals, old peoples' homes, prisons and the like. Institutions constitute an intriguing type of social arena in which food preparation and consumption take place. On the one hand, they are settings which stand in contrast to the public, commercialised world of eating out. On the other, they stand in contrast to home-cooking in the household domain of the personal, private and intimate. At the same time, institutions are to stand in for the domestic sphere, at least in some measure. So the examination of food in institutions has the potential for providing an additional comparative basis for addressing themes such as sociability, exclusion and inclusion in eating which run throughout this report – and are picked up again in the conclusion.

'Institutional' food is the stuff of reminiscences, pleasant and unpleasant; for example, Lambert (1968: 94) reports that in English boarding schools, food aroused the fiercest reaction of any of pupils' daily lives. It features now and then in journalists' exposes of monotony and nutritional inadequacy in British prisons, though it must be noted that this is as nothing to conditions reported elsewhere (for India, see Maguire, 1991). It is also the subject of policy concerns, changes and problems (Platt et al., 1963) and it can figure in surveys of what patients think about hospitals (Cartwright, 1964) and of prisoners' complaints to Boards of Visitors (Maguire and Vagg, 1984). But as Crotty has neatly observed, the 'literature on food and institutionalised people can be divided into two ... [with] *importantly* ... very little overlap' (Crotty, 1988; emphasis added). One deals with dietary needs, nutritional quality of food provided, the influence of medication on nutritional intake and so on. The other, which investigates the social context and organisation of institutional food provision, remains severely under-developed. As the present section seeks to show, this is a worthwhile opportunity missed. For institutions can provide naturally occurring settings in which further to document questions such as control and autonomy in eating.

Goffman's (1968) provocative exposition of 'total institutions' provides us with a framework within which to consider these questions.

Virtually completely enclosed and separated from the wider world, such institutions provide a total and uniform 'living environment' for inmates in which typically their day to day autonomy is limited. No matter whether inmates are confined voluntarily or involuntarily, or whether the institution is designed to care, to punish or to pursue a job of work, patients', internees' or soldiers' spheres of autonomous action are sharply circumscribed compared to those on the outside.

The significance of food appears in different forms according to the type of institution. Studies of life for ship's crews note especially the quality of their food (Fricke, 1972: 127). Indeed, Orbach recounts that the cooking on tuna fishing boats out of San Diego was, 'to say the least, spectacular' (1977: 127) and that skippers would boast to one another over the ships' radios about the excellence of the meals (1977: 30). In these cases, eating is a matter of management's keeping an eye on industrial and human relations, seeking, presumably, to compensate for the restrictions of employment cut off from the sociability of leisure on land. By contrast, institutional food can be used to symbolise the tragedy of an inmate's predicament. For example, the imminent dependency of old age was dreaded by elderly members of a Day Centre, and the disruption to a sense of autonomous adult self encapsulated in the remark that 'in an old age home you can't even make yourself a cup of tea'. But as, the author stresses,

> ... participants acknowledged the fact that tea drinking in itself was not in jeopardy ... What represented the lack of individual autonomy was the inability to perform the ritual of tea making and to select the participants with whom one could share the preparation and the drinking. (Hazan, 1987: 210–11)

As Goffman reminds us, inmates have no say over whom their fellow inmates are to be.

Even those who become inmates by virtue of severe disability strive to sustain a degree of autonomy. Crotty (1988) reports that respirator-dependent patients in an Australian hospital sought and valued freedom of menu choice. Some variation in the hospital menu was available. But it is the significance accorded to items they bought themselves or which were given them by relatives and visitors – homemade foods were especially prized – that both symbolised their autonomy and reaffirmed individual identity and a chink of freedom on visits beyond the ward.

It is not only *what* inmates may do, and in which company, but also *when* they may do it that is beyond their own control. One of the characteristics of total institutions is that the day's activities are tightly scheduled. Moreover, the timing and sequence of activities is imposed organisationally from above. Though one of these activities is bound to be eating, classic studies of timetables in institutions make no (Roth, 1963) or only passing mention of it (Zerubavel, 1979). Ironically, inmates may themselves demand that the expected schedule be strictly adhered to. At the same time, they can be on the lookout for opportunities to demand alternatives to the items served, or seek (in one case of an unscheduled cup of morning coffee for long-term elderly residents) to convert into a right what was initially granted by staff as a favour (Sellerberg, 1991b). Both can be seen as ever-present attempts to challenge the control that lies in the hands of a socially distant supervisory staff and to reclaim some of that control as a means of restoring a sense of the autonomy of normal adulthood.

Only further work in institutions where inmates are not infirm will allow disentangling the consequences of being contained from those of individual incapacity. Moreover, the temptation to conclude that the legitimacy of the freedom to choose what and when people eat is a strong cultural norm will have to be held in check until suitable comparative studies have been mounted.

It is a commonplace of discussions of food and society to speak of the social importance of commensality. Food, and what we do to and with it, is proclaimed to lie at the very core of sociality (Van den Berghe, 1984). A return to the 'classics' reveals similar proclamations. 'Those who eat and drink together are by this very act tied to one another by a bond of friendship and mutual obligation' (Robertson Smith, 1889: 247). Van Gennep notes in his discussion of *rites de passage* that 'the rite of eating and drinking together ... is clearly a rite of incorporation, of physical union ... the sharing of meals is reciprocal, and there is thus an exchange of food which constitutes the confirmation of a bond' (Van Gennep, 1960: 29).

Sharing food is held to signify 'togetherness', an equivalence among a group that defines and reaffirms insiders as socially similar. Feasts cement agreements, treaties and alliances; reconciliations, patching up quarrels, or at least agreeing to differ are sealed in a shared meal – visiting heads of state continually entertain one another at banquets. Safe arrivals, survival and their anniversaries are commemorated by taking special foods together – from Thanksgiving turkey and pumpkin pie in the US, to Cumberland rum butter at baptismal feasts (Williams, 1956), the cake of wedding breakfasts (Wilson, 1973; Charsley, 1987a, 1987b) and funeral meats (Clarke, 1982) as kin groups mark the arrival in, and departure from the group (and this life) of one of their own number.

Familiar examples of special meals that mark group membership readily come to mind – Rotary dinners, English barristers' obligation to dine in their inn of court during the law term, and Women's Institute teas – while the alcoholic drink rather than food of 'hen parties' and 'stag nights' can be seen simultaneously to symbolise membership of, and departure from, all-female or all-male groups. Little sustained or cumulative empirical sociological (as distinct from social anthropological – see Kahn, 1988) – attention has been paid to the analysis of such special occasions, but some is beginning to emerge in allied vein for more mundane versions. For it is not only special meals for special groups that can be approached in this fashion, but also the everyday, routine meals of home, school or workplace, revealing the symbolic significance of eating in the daily round (Murcott, 1982; Batstone, 1983).

Though incompletely investigated, it is highly likely that the meals that are held to be the very stuff of sociality are in danger of disappearing (Burnett, 1989) – part and parcel of the trends characterised earlier in this report as increasing tendencies towards individualisation. A reduction from five meals a day to three in Vienna since the turn of the century and a reorganisation of their type, their timing and an increased likelihood of solo-eating, is shown to be a consequence of the major reorganisation of industrial life (Rotenberg, 1981). Predominantly agricultural until after the Second World War, Finland shows similar changes, but at a slower rate overall, with rural inhabitants continuing to consume two large meals a day where their urban counterparts have reduced to one (Prättälä and Helminen, 1990). These changes, however, need to be set in a longer historical perspective (see Flandrin, 1976, for France; Weatherill, 1988, for Britain) that examines whether, and in which groups, the importance of taking meals together waxes and wanes.

Recognising the importance of commensality is not just an esoteric matter buried in specialist literatures. Functionalist overtones notwith-standing, sociological expressions such as the 'promotion of social solidarity' find an easy equivalence in a modern moral apprehensiveness in the industrialised world. Little documented though often overheard, there seems to be a tendency for those concerned with nutritional adequacy to incorporate a broader anxiety in their reaction to market researchers' reports that taking meals together is being supplanted by 'grazing' on a solitary succession of snacks (Fischler, 1979; Herpin, 1988). The nutritional concern may have some justification: for exam-ple, one study by McIntosh et al. (1990) suggests that old people eating alone tend to be less adequately nourished. Whether the supposed trend away from established patterns of commensality has actually happened is less certain. Worries about the 'decline of the family meal' look as if they are also signalling worries about the 'decline of the family'. Ekström (1991) finds a parallel nostalgic lament for the loss of shared meals of times past among a small group of Swedish adults. She comments, nevertheless, that there is neither evidence for an idyllic past, nor for such widely claimed trends towards solo eating. Public allegiance to the importance of shared meals and the apparent associated tendency toward moral anxiety about their supposed decline deserve closer sociological investigation than they have received so far (Murcott, 1988c) and might well be supported by a harder look at the idea of commensality itself.

For commensality is a perilous notion. If sharing food signifies an equivalence among insiders within a group, it simultaneously defines insiders as socially different from outsiders, and marks the boundary between them (see the discussion of migrant cuisines in Chapter 10). So saying is of a piece with analyses of food habits as 'social markers' (de Garine, 1976), and with the view that rules governing commensality are held to run parallel to rules governing sexual relationships (Douglas, 1975; Goody, 1982).

Inclusion implies exclusion. As Fiddes (1991) notes, those who diverge from common standards risk being stigmatised for their dietary nonconformity. Examples of xenophobic epithets expressed in terms of a revulsion for strangers' consumption of proscribed foodstuffs underscore the point. Not only are Italians 'Macaronis' to Americans, Germans, 'Krauts' and the French 'Frogs' to the English, the Western Lange in the Congo, who eat dogmeat are 'Baschilambua' (dog-people) to the rest of Lange society, and the name 'Dhor', meaning 'eaters of beef' (which is otherwise forbidden) is given to a subgroup of the Katkari caste of Bombay (Goody, 1982: 146).

Okely's (1983) ethnography of gypsies provides a good detailed example. A severely stigmatised and outcast group across Europe, gypsy notions of body, cleanliness and pollution entail a sharp distinction between interior and exterior. Food and eating presents them with difficulties in their already ambivalent relationship with Gorgios, that is, non-Gypsies. Food has commonly to be acquired from Gorgios, those whose own cultural proscriptions for cleanliness are not only at odds with those of Gypsies, but whose structural relation to Gypsy society by definition casts them as unclean. Thus food with such a provenance ever threatens to be polluted, and is continually under suspicion of being deliberately poisoned by Gorgios in yet another attack on Gypsies. Elaborate precautions are taken: the outer crust of a loaf handled during sale by a Gorgio shopkeeper will be removed from the bread, Gypsy men frequenting pubs may take their own beer tankard with them. Far preferable is to stick to eating only among one's own kind, food prepared by Gypsy women themselves. Boundaries are thereby safely marked:

> ... since commensality is a sign of and an affirmation of intimacy, the sharing of eating places with the Gorgio risks not only direct pollution via 'poisoned' food, but also secondary contamination by a weakening of the social boundary between the two groups. (Okely, 1983: 84)

As a reminder that patterns of inclusion and exclusion can change completely, it must also be recalled that formerly despised foods typical of poor and despised groups can become prized and enjoyed: pizzas in the US, the *rijsttafel* in the Netherlands. Nevertheless, as Appadurai (1981) remarks, 'Food in its varied guises, contexts and functions, can signal rank and rivalry, solidarity and community, identity or exclusion, and intimacy or distance'. Appadurai's pointed observation serves as a summary warning to an overemphasis on the analytic and moral virtues of commensality. Societies are notoriously stratified and structured – a theme we have borne in mind throughout this report. And it is more than a matter of 'mere' social patterning or differentiation among human groups, but, as has been seen, inextricably involves questions of power, autonomy and control.

CONCLUSIONS

We have thus returned to where we started: the relation of food to some of the key issues in sociological theory. The discipline of sociology is like a cake: it can be cut up in many different ways. Food and eating have not until very recently generally merited a 'sociology of' to themselves. Even now, the sociology of food and eating is hardly a very unified sub-discipline – if, indeed, it ought to become one. And many, perhaps most, of the sociologists whose work we have reviewed in this report would consider themselves primarily involved in older established fields of interest: comparative-historical sociology, the sociologies of everyday life, the family, of inequality and stratification, or whatever. Nevertheless, as we hope we have shown in this report, the emerging field is one in which the choice of food as a focus makes possible a very wide range of intellectual connections. At one level there are close links to the academic concerns of social anthropologists and historians. At another, where sociologists collaborate with nutritionists or apply nutritional knowledge, there are direct implications for issues of health, social welfare and policy.

In the past, few of the great figures of sociology's classic period paid much direct attention to food and eating per se. For all sorts of reasons – from the increasing convergence of anthropology and sociology, to the rise of the sociology of culture, to concern about hunger in the world today and, above all, perhaps, the increased attention paid to the domestic division of labour through the upsurge of feminist sociology – they have steadily moved closer to the attention of more sociologists.

In consequence, and as a final footnote to this report, it is now possible to point to research networks and centres in the sociology of food developing in a number of countries. Not inappropriately, Paris has perhaps the greatest concentration of talent, with overlapping networks centring on Christiane Grigon, Claude Grignon and Claude Fischler in sociology (besides Pierre Bourdieu), the anthropologist Igor de Garine and the historians Jean-Louis Flandrin and Maurice Aymard. In the Netherlands, there is a focus of more applied research at the Agricultural University of Wageningen. In Germany, Thomas Kutsch heads a federally-funded Institute for Food Economics and Sociology at the Hohenheim University, Stuttgart. In the US, the Association for the Study of Food in Society was formed in 1987, with Bill Whit and William Alex McIntosh among its leading lights. And a Study Group, convened by Teresa Keil and Alan Beardsworth, on the sociology of food and eating was formed within the British Sociological Association in 1991. There is as yet – at least to our knowledge – no journal exclusively devoted to the *sociology* of food and eating, but *Food and Foodways*, edited from Cornell University by the historian Steven Laurence Kaplan, provides an internationally prominent interdisciplinary forum centred on the social sciences and humanities.

Bibliography

ABEL, Wilhelm (1974) *Massenarmut und Hungerkrisen im vorindustriellen Europa: Versuch einer Synopsis*. Hamburg and Berlin: Paul Parey.

ALLEN, D.E. (1968) *British Tastes*. London: Hutchinson.

AMATO, Paul R. and Sonia A. PARTRIDGE (1989) *The New Vegetarians: Promoting Health and Protecting Life*. New York: Plenum Press.

AMERICAN PSYCHIATRIC ASSOCIATION (1980) *Diagnostic and Statistical Manual of Mental Disorders*, 3rd edn. Washington, DC: American Psychiatric Association.

ANDERSON, Eugene N. (1980) '"Heating" and "cooling" foods in Hong Kong and Taiwan', *Social Science Information* 19(2): 237–68.

ANDERSON, Eugene N. (1984) 'Heating and cooling foods re-examined', *Social Science Information* 23(4–5): 755–73.

ANDERSON, Eugene N. (1988) *The Food of China*. New Haven, CT: Yale University Press.

ANON. (1991) 'Ingredients for snack foods'. *Food Technology* 2: 117–19.

APPADURAI, Arjun (1981) 'Gastro-politics in Hindu South Asia', *American Ethnologist* 8(3): 494–511.

ARBER, Sara and Jay GINN (1991) *Gender and Later Life: a sociological analysis of resources and constraints*. London: Sage.

ARNOTT, M.L. (ed.) (1976) *Gastronomy: The Anthropology of Food and Food Habits*. The Hague: Mouton.

ARON, Jean-Paul (1967) *Essai sur la sensibilité alimentaire à Paris au 19ᵉ siècle*. Paris: Armand Colin.

ARON, Jean-Paul (1973) *Le Mangeur du XIXᵉ siècle*. Paris: Robert Laffont. [English translation: *The Art of Eating in France*. London: Peter Owen, 1975].

ARON, Jean-Paul (1979 [orig. 1975]) 'The Art of Using Leftovers: Paris 1850–1900', pp. 98–108 in R. FORSTER and O. RANUM (eds).

ATKINSON, P.A. (1978) 'From honey to vinegar: Levi-Strauss in Vermont', in P. MORLEY and R. WALLIS (eds), *Culture and Curing*. London: Peter Owen.

ATKINSON, P. (1980) 'The symbolic significance of health foods', in M. Turner (ed.).

BACKETT, K. C. (1982) *Mothers and Fathers: a study of the development and negotiation of parental behaviour*. London: Macmillan.

BALAAM, D.M. and M.J. CAREY (eds) (1981) *Food Politics: the Regional Conflict*. London: Croom Helm.

BALL, Daniela (ed.) (1991) *Kaffee im Spiegel europäischer Trinksitten/Coffee in the Context of European Drinking Habits*. Zürich: Johann Jacobs Museum.

BARKER, Diana (1972) 'Young people and their homes: spoiling and "keeping close" in a South Wales town', *Sociological Review* 20: 569–90.

BARKER, M.E. et al. (1988) *Diet, Lifestyle and Health in Northern Ireland*. Coleraine, N. Ireland: Centre for Applied Health Studies, University of Ulster.

BARLÖSIUS, Eva (1988) 'Soziale und historische Aspekte der deutschen Küche', postscript, pp. 423–44, to Stephen MENNELL, *Die Kultivierung des Appetits*. Frankfurt: Athenäum.

BARLÖSIUS, Eva (1989) 'Riechen und Schmecken – Riechendes und Schmeckendes. Ernährungssoziologische Anmerkungen zum Wandel der sinnlichen Wahrnehmung beim Essen, dargestellt an den Beispielen der grande cuisine Frankreichs und der modernen Aromatherstellung', *Kölner Zeitschrift für Soziologie und Sozial-Psychologie*, 39(2): 367–75.

BARTHES, Roland (1957) *Mythologies*. Paris: Seuil.

BARTHES, Roland (1961) 'Pour une psycho-sociologie de l'alimentation contemporaine', *Annales E-S-C* 16(5): 977–86 (English translation: 'Toward a Psychosociology of Contemporary Food Consumption', pp. 166–73 in R. FORSTER and O. RANUM [eds].

BASIOTIS, P., S.R. JOHNSON, K.J. MORGAN, J.S. CHEN (1987) 'Food Stamps, Food Costs, Nutrient Availability and Nutrient Intake', *Journal of Policy Modelling* 9(3): 383–404.

BATSTONE, Eric (1983) 'The Hierarchy of Maintenance and the Maintenance of Hierarchy: Notes on Food and Industry' in A. MURCOTT (ed.).

BEARDSWORTH, A.D. (1990) 'Trans-science and moral panics: understanding food scares', *British Food Journal* 92(5) 11–16.

BELASCO, W.J. (1989) *Appetite for Change. How the Counterculture took on the Food Industry 1966–1988*. New York: Pantheon Books.

BENNION, M., (1976) 'Food preparation in Colonial America', *Journal of the American Dietetic Organisation* July.

BERK, Richard A. and Sarah Fenstermaker BERK (eds) (1979) *Labor and Leisure at Home: Content and Organization of the Household Day*. Beverly Hills, CA: Sage.

BERK, Sarah Fenstermaker and Anthony SMITH (1980) 'Contributions to household labor: comparing wives' and husbands' reports', in S.F BERK (ed.), *Women and Household Labor*. Beverly Hills, CA: Sage.

BHOPAL, R.S. (1986) 'Bhye Bhaddi: a food and health concept of Punjabi Asians', *Social Science and Medicine* 23(7): 687–8.

BLAXTER, Mildred (1979) 'Concepts of causality: lay and medical models', in D.J. OSBORNE, M.M. GRUNEBERG and J.R. EISER (eds), *Research in Psychology and Medicine (2)*. London: Academic Press.

BLAXTER, Mildred (1990) *Health and Lifestyles*. London: Tavistock/Routledge.

BLOOM, Carol (1987) 'Bulimia: A feminist psychoanalytic understanding', pp. 102–14 in M. LAWRENCE (ed.), *Fed Up and Hungry: Women, Oppression and Food*. London: Women's Press.

BLUMER, Herbert (1969) *Symbolic Interactionism: Perspective and Method*. Englewood Cliffs, NJ: Prentice-Hall.

BONNET, Jean-Claude (1986) 'L'Ecriture gourmande de Grimod de la Reynière', *Histoire* 85: 83–6.

BOSE, Christine (1979) 'Technology and the changes in the division of labor in the American home', *Women's Studies International Quarterly* 2(3): 295–304.

BOSERUP, Esther (1983) 'The Impact of Scarcity and Plenty on Development', *Journal of Interdisciplinary History* 14(2): 383–407 (reprinted: pp. 185–209 in R.I. ROTBERG and T.K. RABB [eds]).

BOSKIND-LODAHL, M. (1976) 'Cinderella's stepsisters: A feminist perspective on anorexia and bulimia', *Signs: Journal of Women, Culture and Society* 2: 342–56.

BOTT, Elizabeth (1957) *Family and Social Network*. London: Tavistock.

BOURDIEU, Pierre (1979) *La Distinction*. Paris: le Minuit (English translation: *Distinction: A Social Critique of the Judgement of Taste*. London: Routledge & Kegan Paul, 1986).

BRANNEN, Julia and Gail WILSON (eds) (1987) *Give and Take in Families: studies in resource distribution*. London: Allen & Unwin.

BRAUDEL, Fernand (1979) *Civilisation matérielle, economie et capitalisme, XVe–XVIIIe siècles*, 3 vols. Paris: Armand Colin (English translation: *Civilization and Capitalism, 15th–18th Centuries*. London: Fontana, 1985).

BRAUDEL, Fernand et al. (1961) 'Vie matérielle et comportements biologiques – Bulletin No. 1', *Annales E-S-C* 16(3): 545–74.

BREWER, Stella (1978) *The Forest Dwellers*. London: Collins.

BRINGÉUS, Nils Arvid et al. (eds) (1988) *Wandel der Volkskultur in Europa: Festschrift für Günter Wiegelmann zum 60 Geburtstag (Change in Folk Culture: Festschrift for Günter Wiegelmann on his Sixtieth Birthday)* 2 vols. Münster: Coppenrath Verlag.

BROWN, L.J. (1987) 'Hunger in the U.S.', *Scientific American* 256(2): 37–41.

BROWN, Richard (1976) 'Women as employees: some comments on research in industrial sociology', in D.L. BARKER and S. ALLEN (eds), *Dependence and Exploitation in Work and Marriage*. London: Longman.

BRUCH, Hilde (1973) *Eating Disorders: Obesity, Anorexia Nervosa and the Person Within*. London: Routledge & Kegan Paul.

BRUCH, Hilde (1978) *The Golden Cage: The enigma of anorexia nervosa*. Cambridge, MA: Harvard University Press.

BRUMBERG, Joan J. (1988) *Fasting Girls: The Emergence of Anorexia Nervosa as a Modern Disease*. Cambridge, MA: Harvard University Press.

BRYANT, Carol Anne (1982) 'The impact of kin, friend and neighbor networks on infant feeding practices: Cuban, Puerto Rican and Anglo families in Florida', *Social Science and Medicine* 16: 1757–65.

BRYSON, Lois (1985) 'Gender divisions and power relationships in the Australian family', in Paul CLOSE and Rosemary COLLINS (eds), *Family and Economy in Modern Society*. London: Macmillan.

BURGOYNE, J. and D. CLARK (1983) 'You are what you eat: food and family reconstruction', in Anne MURCOTT (ed.).

BURNETT, John (1966) *Plenty and Want: A Social History of Diet in England from 1815 to the Present Day*. London: Nelson.

BURNETT, John (1979) *Plenty and Want: A Social History of Diet in England from 1815 to the Present Day*. London: Scolar Press, revised edn.

BURNETT, John (1989) *Plenty and Want: A Social History of Diet in England from 1815 to the Present Day*. London: Routledge, third edn.

BUTTON, E.J. and A. WHITEHOUSE (1981) 'Subclinical anorexia nervosa', *Psychological Medicine* 11: 509–16.

CALNAN, M. (1990) 'Food and health: a comparison of beliefs and practices in middle-class and working-class households', in S. CUNNINGHAM-BURLEY and N.P. McKEGANEY (eds), *Readings in Medical Sociology*. London: Tavistock/Routledge.

CALNAN, Michael and Simon WILLIAMS (1991) 'Style of life and the salience of health', *Sociology of Health and Illness* 13(4): 506–29.

CALVO, M. (1982) 'Migration et alimentation', *Information sur les sciences sociales* (21) 3: 383–446.

CARTWRIGHT, Ann (1964) *Human Relations and Hospital Care*. London: Routledge & Kegan Paul.

CASTILLERO-CALVO, A. (1987) 'Nivedas de vida y cambios de dieta a fines del periodo colonial en America' (Standard of living and changes in diet at the end of the colonial period in America), *Anuario de Estudios Americanos* 44: 427–76.

CHAN HO, Suzanne (1985) 'Dietary beliefs in health and illness among a Hong Kong community', *Social Science and Medicine* 20(3): 223–30.

CHANG, Kwang-chih (ed.) (1977) *Food in Chinese Culture: Anthropological and Historical Perspectives*. New Haven, CT: Yale University Press.

CHAPMAN, Malcolm (1990) 'The Social Definition of Want', in CHAPMAN, Malcolm and Helen MACBETH (eds), *Food For Humanity: cross-disciplinary readings*. Oxford: Centre for the Sciences of Food & Nutrition, Oxford Polytechnic.

CHARLES, N. and M. KERR (1986a) 'Eating properly: the family and state benefit', *Sociology* 20(3): 412–29.

CHARLES N. and M. KERR (1986b) 'Food for feminist thought', *Sociological Review* 34(1): 537–72.

CHARLES, Nickie and Marion KERR (1986c) 'Issues of responsibility and control in the feeding of families', in S. RODMELL. and A. WATT (eds), *The Politics of Health Education*. London: Routledge & Kegan Paul.

CHARLES, Nickie and Marion KERR (1987) 'Just the way it is: gender and age differences in family food consumption' in Julia BRANNEN and Gail WILSON (eds).

CHARLES, Nickie and Marion KERR (1988) *Women, Food and Families*. Manchester: Manchester University Press.

CHARSLEY, Simon (1987a) 'Interpretation and custom: the case of the wedding cake', *Man* 22(2): 93–110.

CHARSLEY, S. (1987b) 'What does a wedding cake mean?', *New Society* 81 (3 July): 11–14.

CHERNIN, Kim (1981) *Womansize: the Tyranny of Slenderness*. London: Women's Press.

CHERNIN, Kim (1986) *The Hungry Self*. London: Virago.

CHEYNE, George (1724) *An Essay of Health and Long Life*. London: G. Strachan.

CHEYNE, George (1733) *The English Malady*. London: G. Strachan.

CHIVERS, T.S. (1973) 'The proletarianisation of a service worker', *Sociological Review* 21(4): 633–56.

CHRISTMAN, N. and A. KLEINMAN (1983) 'Popular health care, social networks and cultural meanings', in David MECHANIC (ed.), *Handbook of Health Care and the Health Professions*. New York: Free Press.

CLARISSE, R. (1986) 'L'apéritif, un rituel social', *Cahiers internationaux de sociologie* 80(33): 53–61.

CLARK, D.C. (1982) *Between Pulpit and Pew*. Cambridge: Cambridge University Press.

CLUTTERBUCK, C. and T. LANG (1982) *More than We can Chew: The Crazy World of Food and Farming*. London: Pluto Press.

COATES, Ken and Richard SILBURN (1970) *Poverty: the Forgotten Englishmen*. Harmondsworth: Penguin.

COATES, Ken and SILBURN, Richard (1983) *Poverty: the Forgotten Englishmen*. Nottingham: Spokesman, fourth edn.

COHEN, B.E. (1987) *Hunger in America. Legislative Attitudes in Food Assistance Programs*. Dissertation, Trace University.

COLLINS, Rosemary (1985) '"Horses for Courses": ideology and the division of domestic labour', in Paul CLOSE and Rosemary COLLINS (eds), *Family and Economy in Modern Society*. London: Macmillan.

COMMUNICATIONS (1979) 'Nourriture: Pour une anthropologie bioculturelle de l'alimentation', *Communications* 31, numéro spécial.

COOPER, Eugene (1986) 'Chinese table manners: you are how you eat', *Human Organisation* 45(2): 179–84.

COOPER, P.J. and C.G.FAIRBURN (1983) 'Binge eating and self-induced vomiting in the community – a preliminary study', *British Journal of Psychiatry* 142: 139–44.

COOPER, Peter J., George C. WATERMAN and Christopher G. FAIRBURN (1984), 'Women with eating problems: a community survey', *British Journal of Clinical Psychology* 23(1): 45–52.

CORNWELL, Jocelyn (1984) *Hard-earned Lives – Accounts of Health and Illness from East London.* London: Tavistock.

CORRIGAN, Peter (1989) 'Gender and the gift: the case of the family clothing economy', *Sociology* 23(4): 513–34.

COSMINSKY, S. (1977) 'Alimento and fresco: nutritional concepts nd their implications for health care', *Human Organisation* 36: 203–10.

CRAWFORD, Sir William and H. BROADLEY (1938) *The People's Food.* London: Heinemann.

CRISP, A.H. (1977) 'The prevalence of anorexia nervosa and some of its associations in the general population', *Advances in Psychosomatic Medicine* 9: 38–47.

CROTTY, P. A. (1988) 'The disabled in institutions: transforming functional into domestic modes of food provision', in A.S. TRUSWELL and M.L. WAHLQVIST (eds), *Food Habits in Australia*, Balwyn. Victoria: Rene Gordon.

CURRIER, Richard (1966) 'The hot-cold syndrome and symbolic balance in Mexican and Spanish-American folk medicine', *Ethnology* 5: 251–63.

CURTIS-BENNETT, Sir Noel (1949) *The Food of the People: Being a History of Industrial Eating.* London: Faber & Faber.,

DAMAS, S. (1972) 'Central Eskimo systems of food sharing', *Ethnology* 11: 220–40.

DARE, Salle E. (1988) 'Too many cooks? Food acceptability and women's work in the informal economy', Falmer, Brighton UK: Science Policy Research Unit, University of Sussex, unpublished.

DARKE, Sylvia, J. (1980) 'Nutrition', *Health Visitor* 53(8): 301.

DAS GUPTA, Monica (1987) 'Selective discrimination against female children in rural Punjab, India', *Population and Development Review* 13: 77–100.

DAUREU, F., J. FRIEDLANDER, M. PASQUIER, and J. PRITCHETT (1986) 'La cuisine américaine', *Revue française d'études américaines* 27–28(11): 9–155.

DAVIDSON, Alan (ed.) (1983) *Food in Motion: The Migration of Foodstuffs and Cookery Techniques, Proceedings of the Oxford Cookery Symposium, 1983.* London: Prospect Books.

DAVIES, Margaret Llewellyn (ed.) (1978 [orig. 1915]) *Maternity: Letters from Working Women.* London: Virago.

DAVISON, C., G. DAVEY SMITH and S. FRANKEL (1991) 'Lay epidemiology and the prevention paradox: the implications of coronary candidacy for health education', *Sociology of Health and Illness* 13(1): 1–19.

DAWELL, F. et al. (1986) 'La cuisine Américaine', *Revue Française d'études Américaines* 11: 27–8.

DEEM, Rosemary (1986) *All Work and No Play?: the Sociology of Women and Leisure.* Milton Keynes: Open University Press.

DEJONG, William (1980) 'The stigma of obesity: the consequences of naive assumptions concerning the causes of physical deviance', *Journal of Health and*

Social Behaviour 21: 75–87.

DELPHY, C. (1979) 'Sharing the same table: consumption and the family', in C. HARRIS (ed.), *The Sociology of the Family: new directions for Britain*. Sociological Review Monograph 28, Keele: University of Keele.

DE MAUSE, L. (1974) 'The Evolution of Childhood' in L. DE MAUSE (ed.), *The History of Childhood*. London: Souvenir Press.

DEMBÍNSKA, M. (1986) 'Innovation in food habits – VI Miedzynarodowa Konferencja Etnologicznohistoryczna, Karniowice kolo Krakowa, 2–13 Pazdiernica 1985' (Innovation in food habits: The Sixth International Conference on Ethnology and History, Karniowice near Cracow, 8–13 October 1985), *Kwartalnik Historii Kultury Materialny* 34(2): 390–94.

DEPARTMENT OF HEALTH (UK) (1991) *Dietary Reference Values for Food Energy and Nutrients for the United Kingdom*. London: HMSO.

DETTWYLER, Katherine A. (1987) 'Breastfeeding and weaning in Mali: cultural context and hard data', *Social Science and Medicine* 24(8): 633–44.

DEVAULT, Marjorie L. (1991) *Feeding the Family: the social organisation of caring as gendered work*. Chicago IL: Chicago University Press.

DEVAULT, M. and J.P. PITTS (1984) 'Surplus and scarcity: hunger and the origins of the food stamp program', *Social Problems* 31(5): 545–57.

DHEW. (1981) *Assessing Changing Food Consumption*. Report by the Committee on Food Consumption Patterns on behalf of the Food and Drug Administration, Department of Health, Education and Welfare, Washington. Washington, DC: National Academy Press.

DIEHL, J.M. and C. LEITZMANN (eds) (1986) *Measurement and Determinants of Food Habits and Food Preferences*. Euronutreport No. 7 (E.C. Workshop, 1–4 May 1985) Giessen, West Germany.

DINHAM, B. and G. HINES (1982) *Agribusiness in Africa*. London: Earth Resources Research.

DOAN, Rebecca Miles and Leila BISHARAT (1990) 'Female autonomy and child nutritional status: the extended-family residential unit in Amman, Jordan', *Social Science and Medicine* 31(7): 783–89.

DOBASH, R.E. and R. DOBASH (1980) *Violence Against Wives*. London: Open Books.

DONOVAN, Frances R. (1920) *The Woman who Waits*. Boston: R.G. Badger.

DOUDIET, E. W. (1976) 'Coastal Maine cooking: foods and equipment from 1760', in M.L. ARNOTT (ed.).

DOUGLAS, Mary (1966) *Purity and Danger: an analysis of the concepts of pollution and taboo*. London: Routledge and Kegan Paul.

DOUGLAS, Mary (1972) 'Deciphering a meal', *Dædalus* 101(1): 61–81 (reprinted in *Implicit Meanings: Essays in Anthropology*, pp. 249–75. London: Routledge & Kegan Paul, 1975).

DOUGLAS, Mary (1974) 'Food as an art form', *Studio International* September: 83–8.

DOUGLAS, Mary (1975) *Implicit Meanings*. London: Routledge.

DOUGLAS, Mary (1977) 'Structures of gastronomy', in *The Future and the Past: Annual Report of the Russell Sage Foundation, 1976–77*. New York: Russell Sage Foundation.

DOUGLAS, Mary (1978) 'Culture', pp. 55–81 in *Annual Report of the Russell Sage Foundation, 1977–78*. New York: Russell Sage Foundation.

DOUGLAS, Mary (1984a) *Food in the Social Order: Studies of Food and Festivities in Three American Communities*. New York: Russell Sage Foundation.

DOUGLAS, Mary (1984b) 'Fundamental Issues in Food Problems', *Current Anthropology* 25(4): 498–9.

DOUGLAS, Mary and Jonathan GROSS (1981) 'Food and culture: measuring the intricacy of rule systems', *Social Science Information* 20(1): 1–35.

DOUGLAS, M. and R.S. KHARE (1979) 'Commission on the anthropology of food: statement on its history and current objectives', *Social Science Information* 19: 903–13.

DOUGLAS, Mary and Michael NICOD (1974) 'Taking the biscuit: the structure of British meals', *New Society* 30 (637): 744–7.

DOUGLAS, Mary and Françoise REUMAUX (1988) 'Complexité culturelle: cuisine et société', *Sociétés* 19 (septembre): 6–10.

DRAPER, H.H. (1977) 'The aboriginal Eskimo-Diet in modern perspective', *American Anthropologist* 79: 309–16.

DRIVER, Christopher (1983) *The British at Table, 1940–1980*. London: Chatto and Windus.

DRIVER, Christopher (1984) 'How the poor eat', *New Society* 22 November.

DRUMMOND, Sir Jack and Anne WILBRAHAM (1939) *The Englishman's Food: A History of Five Centuries of English Diet*. London: Jonathan Cape.

DRUMMOND Neil and Christine MASON (1990) 'Diabetes in a social context: just a different way of life in the age of reason', in S. CUNNINGHAM-BURLEY and Neil P. McKEGANEY (eds), *Readings in Medical Sociology*. London: Tavistock/Routledge.

DUHL, L.J., J.D. KLEIN and M.R. HALL (1985) 'The food system in California: trouble in the golden state', *Ecology of Food and Nutrition* 17: 205–17.

DURKHEIM, Emile (1912) *Les formes élémentaires de la vie religieuse*. Paris: Alacan (English translation: *The Elementary Forms of the Religious Life*. London: Allen & Unwin, 1915).

DURKHEIM, Emile and Marcel MAUSS (1963 [orig. 1903]) *Primitive Classification*. London: Cohen & West.

DYHOUSE, Carol (1977) 'Good wives and little mothers: social anxieties and the schoolgirl's curriculum, 1890–1920', *Oxford Review of Education* 3(1): 21–33.

EDGELL, S. (1980) *Middle Class Couples: a study of segregation, domination and inequality in marriage*. London: Allen and Unwin.

EDWARDS, P., A.C. ACOCK, and R.L. JOHNSTON (1985) 'Nutrition behavior change: outcomes of an educational approach', *Evaluation Review* 9(4): 441–59.

EICHINGER FERRO-LUZZI, G. (1980) 'Food avoidance of pregnant women in Tamiland', in J.R.K. ROBSON (ed.).

EKSTRÖM, Marianne (1991) 'Class and gender in the kitchen' in Elisabeth FÜRST et al. (eds), *Palatable Worlds: sociocultural food studies*. Oslo: Solum Forlag.

ELIAS, Norbert (1978/82 [orig.1939]) *The Civilising Process*, Vol. I, *The History of Manners* and Vol.II, *State Formation and Civilisation* (US title: *Power and Civility*). Oxford, Basil Blackwell.

ELIAS, Norbert (1983 [orig. 1969]) *The Court Society*. Oxford: Blackwell.

ELLERBROCK, K. (1987) 'Lebensmittelqualität vor dem Ersten Weltkrieg: Industrielle Produktion und staatliche Gesundheitspolitik', pp. 127–89 in H.J. TEUTEBERG (ed.).

ELLIS, R. (1983) 'The Way to a Man's Heart: Food in the Violent Home', pp. 164–71 in A. MURCOTT (ed.).

ENGELS, Friedrich (1969 [orig. 1845]) *The Condition of the Working Class in England.* London: Granada.

ENGSTRÖM, A. (1984) 'Reflexioner krieg vara matvanor förr och nu' (Some observations on eating habits then and now), pp. 83–90 in *Nordisk Medecinhistorisk Arsbok 1984.*

ERASMUS, Desiderius (*c.* 1518) *Twenty Select Colloquies of Erasmus.* London: Chapman and Dodd, n.d.

ESSEMYR, Mats (1986) 'Food, fare and nutrition: some reflections on the historical development of food consumption', *Scandinavian Economic History Review* 34(2): 76–89.

FALLON, A.E. and P. ROZIN (1985) 'Sex differences in perceptions of desirable body shape', *Journal of Abnormal Psychology* 94: 102–5.

FARB, Peter and George ARMELAGOS (1980) *Consuming Passions: The Anthropology of Eating.* Boston: Houghton Mifflin.

FARMER, A., J. TREASURE and G. SZMUKLER (1986) 'Eating disorders: a review of recent research', *Digestive Diseases* pp. 13–25.

FARRER, K.T.H. (1980) *A Settlement Amply Supplied: Food Technology in Nineteenth-Century Australia.* Melbourne: Melbourne University Press.

FARRER, K.T.H. (1983) *Fancy Eating That! A closer look at food additives and contaminants.* Melbourne, Melbourne University Press.

FENTON, A. and T.M. OWEN (eds) (1977) *Food in Perspective: Proceedings of the Third International Conference on Ethnological Food Research.* Edinburgh: John Donald.

FENTON, A. and E. KISBÁN (eds) (1986) *Food in Change: Eating Habits from the Middle Ages to the Present Day.* Edinburgh: John Donald.

FIDDES, Nick (1991) *Meat: a Natural Symbol.* London: Routledge.

FIELD, R. (1984) *Irons in the Fire: A History of Cooking Equipment.* London: Crowood Press.

FINCH, J. (1983) *Married to the Job: Wives' Incorporation in Men's Work,* London: Allen & Unwin.

FINCH, J. (1987) 'Age', in R.G. BURGESS (ed.), *Key Variables in Social Investigation.* London: Routledge & Kegan Paul.

FINCH, Janet and Dulcie GROVES (1983) *A Labour of Love.* London: Routledge & Kegan Paul.

FINE, Gary Alan (1985) 'Occupational Æsthetics: How Trade School Students Learn to Cook', *Urban Life* 14(1): 3–31.

FINE, Gary Alan (1987) 'Working Cooks: The Dynamics of Professional Kitchens', *Current Research on Occupations and Professions* 4: 141–58.

FINE, Gary Alan (forthcoming) 'The Culture of Production: Aesthetic Choices and Constraints in Culinary Work', *American Journal of Sociology.*

FINK, Ann Elizabeth (1985) 'Nutrition, lactation and fertility in two Mexican rural communities', *Social Science and Medicine* 20(12): 1295–305.

FINKELSTEIN, Joanne (1985) 'Dining out: the self in search of civility', *Studies in Symbolic Interaction* 6: 183–212.

FINKELSTEIN, Joanne (1989) *Dining Out: A Sociology of Modern Manners.* Cambridge: Polity.

FISCHLER, Claude (1979) 'Gastro-nomie et gastro-anomie: Sagesse du corps et crise bioculturelle de l'alimentation moderne', *Communications* 31: 189–210.

FISCHLER, Claude (1980) 'Food habits, social change and the nature/culture dilemma', *Social Science Information* 19(6): 937–53.

FISCHLER, Claude (1985) 'Alimentation, cuisine et identité: l'identification des aliments et l'identité du mangeur', *Recherches et traveaux de l'Institut d'Ethnologie* 6: 171–92.

FISCHLER, Claude (1986a) 'Learned versus "spontaneous" dietetics: French mothers' views of what children should eat', *Social Science Information* 25(4): 945–65.

FISCHLER, Claude (1986b) 'Food likes, dislikes and some of their correlates in a sample of French children and young adults', in J.M. DIEHL and C. LEITZMANN (eds).

FISCHLER, Claude (1988) 'Food, self and identity', *Social Science Information* 27(2): 275–92.

FISCHLER, Claude (1989) 'Cuisines and food selection', pp. 193–206 in D.M.H. THOMSON (ed.), *Food Acceptability*. London: Elsevier.

FISCHLER, Claude (1990) *L'Homnivore: le goût, la cuisine et le corps*. Paris: Éditions Odile Jacob.

FISHMAN, C., R. EVANS and E. JENKS (1988) 'Warm bodies, cool milk: conflicts in post partum food choice for Indochinese women in California', *Social Science and Medicine* 26(11): 1125–32.

FISHMAN, P.B. (1985) 'Teaching consumers about food purchasing and ecology', *Ecology of Food and Nutrition* 16: 33–7.

FITCHEN, J.M. (1988) 'Hunger, malnutrition and poverty in the contemporary United States: Some observations on their social and cultural context', *Food and Foodways* 2: 309–33.

FITZGERALD, T.E. (ed.) (1976) *Nutrition and Anthropology in Action*. Assen: Van Gorcum.

FLANDRIN, Jean-Louis (1976) *Families in Former Times*. Cambridge: Cambridge University Press.

FLETCHER, R. (1962) *The Family and Marriage: an analysis and moral assessment*. Harmondsworth: Penguin.

FLINT, Delia M. (1982) 'The elderly', in Mark L. WAHLQVIST (ed.), *Food and Nutrition in Australia*. North Ryde, NSW: Methuen.

FOOD AND NUTRITION BOARD, National Research Council (1981) *Assessing Changing Food Consumption Patterns*. Washington DC: National Academy Press.

FORSTER, Elborg and Robert FORSTER (eds) (1975) *European Diet from Preindustrial to Modern Times*. New York: Harper & Row.

FORSTER, Robert and Orest RANUM (eds) (1979) *Food and Drink in History: selections from the Annales E-S-C*. Baltimore: Johns Hopkins University Press.

FORTES, M. and S.L. FORTES (1936) 'Food in the Domestic Economy of the Tallensi', *Africa* 9: 237–76.

FOSTER, George M. and F.K. KAFERSTEIN (1985) 'Food safety and the behavioural sciences', *Social Science and Medicine* 21(11): 1273–77.

FOX, B. (1980) *Hidden in the Household: Women's Domestic Labour Under Capitalism*. Toronto: Women's Educational Press.

FREEDMAN, M.R. and L.E. GRIVETTI (1984) 'Diet patterns of first, second and third generation Greek-American women', *Ecology of Food and Nutrition* 14: 185–204.

FREEDMAN, R.L. (1977) 'Nutritional anthropology: an overview', in T.E. Fitzgerald (ed.).

FRICKE, P. (1972) 'The social structure of the crews of British dry cargo merchant ships: a study of the organisation and environment of an occupation', Cardiff: UWIST Department of Maritime Studies.

FRIEDAN, B. (1965) *The Feminine Mystique*. Harmondsworth: Penguin.

FRIJHOFF, Willem (1988) 'De volkskunde herplaatst tussen geschiedenis en antropologie: Een evaluatie van Voskuils werk' (Ethnology placed between history and anthropology: an evaluation of Voskuyil's work), *Volkskundig Bulletin* 14: 45–54.

GAMARNIKOW, E. et al. (eds) (1983) *The Public and the Private*. London: Heinemann.

GARFINKEL, P.E. and D.M. GARNER (1982) *Anorexia Nervosa: A Multidimensional Perspective*. New York: Brunner/Mazel.

GARINE, Igor de (1976) 'Food, tradition and prestige', in D. WALCHER et al. (eds), *Food, Man and Society*. New York: Plenum Press.

GARINE, Igor de (1980) 'Approaches to the study of food and prestige in Savannah tribes – Massa and Mussey of northern Cameroon and Chad', *Social Science Information* 19(10): 39–78.

GARINE, Igor de and Sjors KOPPERT (1990) 'Social adaptation to season and uncertainty in food supply', in C.A. HARRISON and J.C. WATERLOW (eds), *Diet and Disease in Traditional and Developing Societies*. Cambridge: Cambridge University Press.

GARNER, D.M., P.E. GARFINKEL, D. SCHWARTZ and M. THOMPSON (1980) 'Cultural expectations of thinness in women', *Psychological Reports* 47: 483–491.

GARNSEY, P. (1990) *Famine and Food Supply in the Graeco-Roman World: Responses to Risk and Crisis*. Cambridge: Cambridge University Press.

GAVRON, H. (1966) *The Captive Wife: Conflicts of Housebound Mothers*. London: Routledge & Kegan Paul.

GENNEP, Arnold van (1909) *Les Rites de passage*. Paris: Nourry (English translation: *The Rites of Passage*. London: Routledge & Kegan Paul, 1960).

GEORGE, Susan (1986) 'The right to food and the politics of hunger', *Razvoj. International Development* 1(1): 121–37.

GERSHUNY, J.I. (1982) 'Livelihood IV: household tasks and the use of time', in Sandra WALLMAN (ed.), *Living in South London*. Aldershot: Gower.

GERSHUNY, J.I. and R.E. PAHL (1983) 'Britain in the decade of the three economies', *New Society* 3 January: 7–9.

GEX-FABRY, M. et al. (1988) 'Multivariate analysis of dietary patterns in 939 Swiss adults: sociodemographic parameters and alcohol consumption profiles', *International Journal of Epidemiology* 17: 548–55.

GIEDION, S. (1975 [orig. 1948]) *Mechanization Takes Command: A Contribution to Anonymous History*. New York: W.W. Norton.

GIOBELLINA-BRUMANA, F. (1988) 'La comida de santo en el candomble' (The sacred meal in the Candomble cult), *Americ Indigena* 48(3): 605–17.

GOFFMAN, Erving (1968) *Asylums*. Harmondsworth: Penguin.

GOFFMAN, Erving (1971 [orig. 1959]) *The Presentation of Self in Everyday Life*. Harmondsworth: Penguin.

GOFTON, Leslie (1983) 'Real ale and real men', *New Society*, 17 November: 271–3.

GOFTON Leslie (1990) 'Food fears and time famines: some social aspects of choosing and using food', *The British Nutrition Foundation Nutrition Bulletin* 15(1): 79–95.

GOLD, M. (1983) *Assault and Battery*. London: Pluto Press.

GOODY, Jack (1968) *Literacy in Traditional Societies*. Cambridge: Cambridge University Press.

GOODY, Jack (1977) *The Domestication of the Savage Mind*. Cambridge: Cambridge University Press.

GOODY, Jack (1982) *Cooking, Cuisine and Class: A Study in Comparative Sociology*. Cambridge: Cambridge University Press.

GOUDSBLOM, Johan (1992) *Fire and Civilisation*. Harmondsworth: Allen Lane.

GOULD-MARTIN, Katherine (1978) 'Hot cold clean poison and dirt: Chinese folk medical categories', *Social Science and Medicine* 12: 39–46.

GOVE, W.R. and J.F. TUDOR (1973) 'Adult sex roles and mental illness', *American Journal of Sociology* 78: 812–35.

GRAHAM, Hilary (1979) '"Prevention and health: every mother's business": a comment on child health policies in the 1970s', in C. HARRIS (ed.), *The Sociology of the Family: new directions for Britain*. Sociological Review Monograph 28, Keele: University of Keele.

GRAHAM, Hilary (1984) *Women, Health and the Family*. Brighton: Wheatsheaf.

GRIGNON, Claude (1981) 'Alimentation et stratification sociale', *Cahiers de nutrition et de diététique* 16(4): 207–17.

GRIGNON, Claude (1985) 'Nos habitudes alimentaires sont-elles en train de changer?', *L'Histoire* 85: 128–34.

GRIGNON, Claude (1986) *Les clientèles du restaurant universitaire*. Paris: INRAC-NOUS.

GRIGNON, Claude (1987) *L'Alimentation des étudiants*. Paris: INRA.

GRIGNON, Claude (1988) 'Les enquêtes sur la consommation et la sociologie des goûts', *Revue economique* 1: 15–32.

GRIGNON, Claude (1989) 'Hierarchical cuisine or standard cooking?', *Food and Foodways* 3(3): 177–83.

GRIGNON, Claude and Christiane GRIGNON (1980) 'Styles d'alimentation et goûts populaires', *Revue française de sociologie* 21(4): 531–69.

GRIGNON, Claude and Christiane GRIGNON (1984) 'Les pratiques alimentaires', pp. 336–39 in *Données Sociales*, 5th edn. Paris: INSEE.

GRIGNON, Claude and Christiane GRIGNON (1986a) 'Pratiques alimentaires et classes sociales: des différences importantes', *Problèmes politiques et sociaux* 544: 22–7.

GRIGNON, Claude and Christiane GRIGNON (1986b) 'Alimentation et stratification sociale', *Cahiers de nutrition et de diététique* 16(4): 207–17.

HABERMAS, Jürgen (1962) *Strukturwandel der Öffentlichkeit*. Neuwied: Luchterhand (English translation: *The Structural Transformation of the Public Sphere*. Cambridge: Polity Press).

HAMBLIN, Douglas (1980) 'Adolescent attitudes towards food', in M. TURNER (ed.).

HARALDSDOTTIR, J. et al. (1987) *Danskernes kosvvanen 1985: 2. Hvem spiser hvad?* (Dietary Habits in Denmark 1985: 2. Who Eats What?). Soberg: Levueds middelstyrelsen.

HARPER, A.E. (1988) 'Killer French fries: the misguided drive to improve the American diet', *Sciences* 28(1): 21–7.

HARRELL-BOND, B.E. (1969) 'Conjugal role behaviour', *Human Relations* 22(1): 77–91.

HARRINGTON, Michael (1963) *The Other America: Poverty in the United States*. Harmondsworth: Penguin.

HARRIS, C.C. and L. MORRIS (1986) 'Households, labour markets and the position of women', in R. CROMPTON and M. MANN (eds), *Gender and Stratification*. Cambridge: Polity.

HARRIS, Marvin B. (1986) *Good to Eat: Riddles of Food and Culture*. New York: Simon & Schuster.

HARRIS, M.B., K.M. KOEHLER and S.M. DAVIS (1984) 'Food intake in a multicultural southwestern population ii. Ethnic, gender and age distributions', *Ecology of Food and Nutrition* 21: 287–96.

HARRISS Barbara (1990) 'Food distribution, death and disease in South Asia', in G.A. HARRISON and J.C. WATERLOW (eds), *Diet and Disease in Traditional and Developing Societies*. Cambridge: Cambridge University Press.

HART, K. and T.H. OLLENDIECK (1985) 'Prevalence of bulimia in working and university women', *American Journal of Psychiatry* 142: 851–4.

HARTNETT, O. et al. (eds) (1979) *Women: sex-role stereotyping*. London: Tavistock.

HARTOG, A.J. den (1980) 'De beginfase van het moderne voedselpatroon in Nederland. Voedsel en voeding in de jaren 1850–1914 – een verkenning, I en II', *Voeding* 41(9): 334–42; 41(10): 348–56.

HARTOG, A. P. den (1986) *Diffusion of Milk as a New Food to Tropical Regions: the Example of Indonesia 1880–1942*. Wageningen: Stichting Voeding Nederland.

HAYDEN, Dolores (1978) 'Two Utopian feminists and their campaigns for kitchenless houses', *Signs* 4(2): 274–90.

HAZAN, H. (1987) 'Holding time still with cups of tea' in M. DOUGLAS (ed.), *Constructive Drinking: perspectives on drink from anthropology*. Cambridge: Cambridge University Press.

HEAL, Felicity (1990) *Hospitality in Early Modern England*. Oxford: Clarendon Press.

HELMAN, Cecil (1978), '"Feed a cold, starve a fever": folk models of infection in an English suburban community', *Culture, Medicine and Psychiatry* 2: 107–37.

HÉMARDINQUER, J.J. (ed.) (1970) *Pour une histoire de l'alimentation*. Paris: Armand Colin.

HÉMARDINQUER, J.J. (1979 [orig. 1970]) 'The family pig of the ancien régime: myth or fact', pp. 50–72 in R. FORSTER and O. RANUM (eds).

HERPIN, N. (1984) 'Panier et budget: l'alimentation des ouvriers urbains', *Revue française de sociologie* 25: 20–48.

HERPIN, N. (1988) 'Le repas comme institution: Compte rendu d'un enquête exploratoire', *Revue française de sociologie* 29: 503–21.

HERZLICH, C. (1973) *Health and Illness: a Social Psychological Analysis*. London: Academic Press.

HILLIARD, S. (1969) 'Hogmeat and cornpone: food habits in the Ante Bellum South', *Proceedings of the American Philosophical Society* 113(1).

HILLIARD, S. (1972) *Hogmeat and Hoe Cake: Food Supply in the Old South*. Illinois: Southern Illinois University Press.

HODES, Matthew (1991) 'Food for thought: issues for the social anthropology of eating disorders', unpublished ms.

HOMANS, Hilary (1983) 'A question of balance: Asian and British women's perceptions of food during pregancy', pp. 73–83 in Anne MURCOTT (ed.).

HONKASALO, Marja-Liisa (1989) ' "Have the wives over for a sauna when I go out with the men!"', pp. 76–96 in Salme AHLSTROM and Elina HAAVIO-MANNILA (eds) *Women, Alcohol and Drugs in the Nordic Countries*. Helsinki: NAD publications.

HORSFALL, Jan (1991): 'The silent participant: Bryan Turner on anorexia nervosa', *Australian and New Zealand Journal of Sociology* 27(2): 232–4.

HUBER, Joan and Glenna SPITZE (1983) *Sex Stratification: Children, Housework and Jobs*. New York: Academic Press.

HUNG, Beatrice K.M., Lydia LING and S.G. ONG (1985) 'Sources of influence on infant feeding practices in Hong Kong', *Social Science and Medicine* 20(11): 1143–50.

HUNT, Pauline (1980) *Gender and Class Consciousness*. London: Macmillan.

HUTTER, Mark (1970) 'Summertime servants: The Schlockhaus waiter', pp. 203–25 in Glenn JACOBS (ed.), *The Participant Observer*. New York: George Braziller.

IGUN, U.A. (1982) 'Child-feeding habits in a situation of social change: the case of Maiduguri, Nigeria', *Social Science and Medicine* 16: 769–81.

ILMONEN, K (1991) 'Change and stability in Finnish eating habits', in Furst et al. (eds), *Palatable Worlds: Sociocultural Food Studies*. Oslo: Solum.

JAKOBSON, R. (1988) 'Le Brochet à la polonaise', *Sociétés* 19(Sept.): 11–16.

JAMES, A. (1981) 'Confections, concoctions and conceptions', in A. Waites *et al.* (eds), *Popular Culture Past and Present*. London: Croom Helm.

JAMES, Allison and Alan PROUT (1990) *Constructing and Reconstructing Childhood: contemporary issues in the sociological study of childhood*, Basingstoke: Falmer Press.

JEROME, N.W. (1975) 'On determining food patterns of urban dwellers in contemporary United States society', in M. ARNOTT (ed.).

JEROME N.W., R.F. KANDEL and G.H. PELTO (eds) (1980) *Nutritional Anthropology. Contemporary Approaches to Diet and Culture*. New York: Redgrave.

JOBSE-van PUTTEN, J. (1989) *Van pekelvat tot diepvrieskist. Interviews en beschouwingen over de huishoudelijke conservering op het Nederlandse platteland in de eerste helft van de twintigste eeuw* (From pickle-tub to freezer: Interviews and observations on household preservation in the Dutch countryside in the first half of the twentieth century). Amsterdam: Meertens-Instituut.

JOHNSON, G.D. (1986) 'A world food system: actuality or promise?', *Perspectives in Biology and Medicine* 29(2): 180–98.

JONES, Dee A. (1986) 'Attitudes of breast-feeding mothers; a survey of 649 mothers', *Social Science and Medicine* 23(11): 1151–6.

KAHN, Miriam (1988) '"Men are taro" (They cannot be rice): political aspects of food choices in Wamira, P.N.G.', *Food and Foodways* 3(1+2): 41–58.

KANDEL, R.F. and G.H. PELTO (1980) 'The health food movement: social revitalisation or alternative health maintenance system?' in N.W. Jerome, R.F. KANDEL and G.H. PELTO (eds), *Nutritional Anthropology: Contemporary Approaches to Diet and Culture*. New York: Redgrave.

KAPFERER, J.N. (1985) 'Une humeur de poison chez les Français: le tracht de collejuif', *Communications* 11(1): 111–19.

KAPLAN, Steven L. (1984) *Provisioning Paris: Merchants and Millers in the Grain and Flour Trade during the Eighteenth Century*. Ithaca: Cornell University Press.

KEIL, Teresa and Alan BEARDSWORTH (1991) 'Contemporary vegetarianism: eating from a moral menu?', unpublished paper presented at the British Sociological Annual Conference, University of Manchester, UK.

KELPP-KNUT, I. and J.L. FORSTER (1985) 'The Norwegian nutrition and food policy: an integrated policy approach to a public health problem', in *Journal of Public Health Policy* 6(4): 447–63.

KERR, Marion and Nickie CHARLES (1982) 'Food as an indicator of social relations', unpublished paper presented at the British Sociological Association Annual Conference, University of Manchester, UK.

KERR Marion and Nickie CHARLES (1986) 'Servers and providers: the distribution of food within the family', *Sociological Review* 34(3): 115–57.

KHARE, R.S. (1980) 'Food as nutrition and culture: notes towards an anthropological methodology', *Social Science Information* 19(3): 519–42.

KING, J. and A. ASHWORTH (1987) 'Historical review of the changing pattern of infant feeding in developing countries: the case of Malaysia, the Caribbean, Nigeria and Zaïre', *Social Science and Medicine* 25(12): 1307–20.

KING, S. (1979) 'Presentation and the choice of food', in M. TURNER (ed.).

KISBÁN, Esther (1986) 'Food habits in change: the example of Europe', pp. 2–11 in A. FENTON and E. KISBÁN (eds).

KLEINMAN, A. (1980) *Patients and Healers in the Context of Culture*, Berkeley: University of California Press.

KOO, Linda C. (1984) 'The use of food to treat and prevent disease in Chinese culture', *Social Science and Medicine* 18(9): 757–66.

KOSHI, Ryoko (1988) 'Preferences and perceived social norms for division of work and family responsibilities among Japanese college students', *Psychological Reports* 63: 403–6.

KRONDL, M. and P. COLEMAN (1986) 'Social and Biocultural determinants of food selection', *Progress in Food and Nutrition science* 10: 179–203.

KROPOTKIN, Piotr (1972 [orig. 1892]) *The Conquest of Bread*. London: Allen Lane, The Penguin Press.

KUMAR, V. et al. (1981) 'Maternal beliefs regarding diet during acute diarrhoea', *Indian Journal of Paediatrics* 48: 599–603.

KUTSCH, Thomas (1986) 'Soziale Determinanten und Rahmenbedingungen des Ernä hrungsverhaltens' [Social determinants and delimiting conditions of nutritional behaviour], *Hauswirtschaft und Wissenschaft* 34(1): 5–15.

KUTSCH, Thomas (1990) 'Ethnic food, cuisines réegionales, gruppen- und landschafts- typische Küchen: Essen als Teil der sozialen Identität', *Ernährungs-Umschau* 37(Beiheft): 29–37.

LACEY, Richard (1989) *Safe Shopping, Safe Cooking, Safe Eating*. Harmondsworth: Penguin.

LACEY, Richard (1991) *Unfit for Human Consumption: Food in Crisis: the consequences of putting profit before safety*. London: Souvenir.

LADERMAN, Carol (1984) 'Food ideology and eating behavior: contributions from Malay studies', *Social Science and Medicine*, 19(5): 547–59.

LAITE, Julian and Peter HALFPENNY (1987) 'Employment, unemployment and the domestic division of labour', in D. FRYER and P. ULLAH (eds), *Unemployed People: Social and Psychological Perspectives*. Milton Keynes: Open University Press.

LAMBERT, Royston (1968) *The Hothouse Society: an Exploration of Boarding-school Life through the Boys' and Girls' Own Writings*. London: Weidenfeld & Nicolson.

LAND, H. (1977) 'Inequalities in large families: more of the same or different', in R. CHESTER and J. PEEL (eds), *Equalities and Inequalities in Family Life*. New York: Academic Press.

LAWRENCE, Marilyn (1984) *The Anorexic Experience*. London: Women's Press.

LAWRENCE, Roderick J. (1982) 'Domestic space and society: a cross-cultural study', *Comparative Studies in Society and History* 24(1): 104–30.

134 *The Sociology of Food*

LECLANT, Jean (1979 [orig. 1951]) 'Coffee and Cafés in Paris, 1640–1693', pp. 86–97 in R. FORSTER and O. RANUM (eds). *Health Visitor* 53(8): 301.

Le GROS CLARK, F. (1945) 'Allocation of food within the family', *Proceedings of the Nutrition Society* 3: 12–15.

LEONARD, D.L. (1980) *Sex and Generation*. London: Tavistock.

LEOPOLD, M. (1985) 'The transnational food companies and their global strategies', *International Social Science Journal* 37(3): 315–30.

LESITSCHNIG, E. (1989) *Nahrung im Wandel. Eine Mikrostudie über Verä nderungen der Nahrungskultur seit 1945 am Beispiel des Ortes St. Margarethen o.T., in Kärnten.* Vienna: Österreichische Nationalbibliothek.

LEVENSTEIN, Harvey A. (1985) 'The American response to Italian food, 1880–1930', *Food and Foodways* 1(1): 1–24.

LEVENSTEIN, Harvey A. (1988) *Revolution at the Table: The Transformation of the American Diet*. New York: Oxford University Press.

LÉVI-STRAUSS, Claude (1963 [orig. 1958]) *Structural Anthropology*. New York: Basic Books.

LÉVI-STRAUSS, Claude (1964) *Le cru et le cuit: Mythologiques I*. Paris: Plon (English translation: *The Raw and the Cooked*. Jonathan Cape, 1969).

LÉVI-STRAUSS, Claude (1965) 'Le triangle culinaire', *L'Arc* 26: 19–29 (English translation: 'The culinary triangle', *Partisan Review* 33, 1966: 586–95).

LÉVI-STRAUSS, Claude (1968) *L'Origine des manières de table: Mythologiques III*. Paris: Plon (English translation: *The Origin of Table Manners*. Jonathan Cape, 1978).

LEWIN, Kurt (1943) 'Forces behind food habits and methods of change', pp. 35–65 in *The Problem of Changing Food Habits*. Bulletin No. 108. Washington, DC: National Academy of Science, National Research Council.

LIPPE-STOKES, S. (1980) 'Eskimo story-knife tales: reflections of change in food habits', pp. 75–82 in K. ROBSON (ed.), *Food, Ecology and Culture*. New York: London: Gordon and Breach.

LITTLE, M. (1991) 'Imperialism, colonialism and the new science of nutrition: the Tanganyika experience', *Social Science and Medicine* 32(1): 11–14.

LITTLEJOHN, James (1963) *Westrigg: the Sociology of a Cheviot Parish*. London: Routledge & Kegan Paul.

LLEWELYN DAVIES, Margaret (1978 [orig. 1915]) *Maternity: Letters from Working Women*. London: Virago.

LOGAN, M.H. and W.T. MORRIL (1979) 'Humoral medicine and informant variability: an analysis of acculturation and cognitive change among Guatamalan villagers', *Human Organization* 38(4): 785–802.

LOPATA, H.Z. (1971) *Occupation: Housewife*. New York: Oxford University Press.

LOVEDAY, L. and S. CHIBA (1985) 'Partaking with the divine and symbolizing the societal: The semiotics of Japanese food and drink', *Semiotics* 56(1–2): 115–31.

LÖWE, Heinz-Dietrich (1986) 'Teuerungsrevolten, Teuerungspolitik und Markt-regulierung im 18. Jahrhundert in England, Frankreich und Deutschland (Food revolts, food policy and market regulation in the eighteenth century in England, France and Germany) *Saeculum* 37(3–4): 291–312.

LOWE, M. (1979) 'Influence of changing lifestyles on food choice', in M. TURNER (ed.).

LUXTON, M. (1980) *More Than a Labour of Love: three generations of women's work in the home*. Toronto: Women's Educational Press.

McINTOSH, W. Alex (1988) 'Chocolate and loneliness among the elderly', paper presented at symposium on 'Chocolate: Food for the Gods'.

McINTOSH, W. Alex and Peggy A. SHIFFLETT (1984) 'Dietary behaviour, dietary adequacy, and religious social support: an exploratory study', *Review of Religious Research* 26(2).

McINTOSH, W. Alex, Peggy A. SHIFFLETT and J. Steven PICOU (1989) 'Social support, stressful events, strain, dietary intake, and the elderly', *Medical Care* 27(2): 140–53.

McINTOSH, W. Alex and Mary ZEY (1989) 'Women as gatekeepers of food consumption: a sociological critique', *Food and Foodways* 34(4): 317–32.

McINTOSH, W. Alex, C. TORRES, K.S. KUBENA and W.A. LANDMANN (1990) 'Mealtime companionship, health and nutrition, and background factors', unpublished typescript.

MACINTYRE, Sally (1983) 'The management of food in pregnancy' in MURCOTT, A. (ed.).

McKENZIE, J.C. (1963) 'Recipes and the housewife', *Home Economics* 9(3): 16–17.

McKENZIE, J.C. (1979) 'Economic influences on food choice', in M. TURNER (ed.).

McKEOWN, Thomas (1977) *The Modern Rise of Population.* London: Edward Arnold.

MacLEOD, Sheila (1981) *The Art of Starvation.* London: Virago.

MAGUIRE, M. (1991) 'The Indian prison', in R. WHITFIELD (ed.), *State of the Prisons: Two Hundred Years On.* London: Routledge.

MAGUIRE, M. and J.VAGG (1984) *The 'Watchdog' Role of Boards of Visitors.* London: The Home Office.

MAINARDI, P. (1980) 'The politics of housework' in E. MALOS (ed.), *The Politics of Housework.* New York: Schocken Books.

MAFF (Ministry of Agriculture, Fisheries and Food, UK) (Annual, 1951–) *Household Food Consumption and Expenditure.* London: HMSO.

MALTHUS, Thomas (1798) *An Essay on the Principle of Population.* London: J. Johnson (Modern edition: Harmondsworth: Penguin, 1970).

MANDERSON, Leonore (1981) 'Traditional food beliefs and critical life events in Peninsular Malaysia', *Social Science Information* 20(6): 947–75.

MANDERSON, Leonore (1984) '"These are modern times": infant feeding practice in peninsular Malaysia', *Social Science and Medicine* 18(1): 47–57.

MANDERSON, Leonore (1987) 'Hot-cold food and medical theories: overview and introduction', *Social Science and Medicine* 25(4): 329–30.

MANSFIELD, Penny and Jean COLLARD (1988) *The Beginning of the Rest of Your Life?.* London: Macmillan.

MASON, Jennifer (1987) 'A bed of roses? women, marriage and inequality in later life', in P. ALLATT et al. (eds), *Women and the Life Cycle.* London: Macmillan.

MARS, Gerald and Michael NICOD (1984) *The World of Waiters.* London: Allen & Unwin.

MARCHIONE, Thomas J. (1984) 'Evaluating primary health care and nutrition programs in the context of national development', *Social Science and Medicine* 19(3): 225–35.

MARSHALL, Gordon (1986) 'The workplace culture of a licensed restaurant', *Theory, Culture and Society* 3(1): 33–47.

MARTIN, J. (1978) *Infant Feeding 1975: attitudes and practice in England and Wales.* London: OPCS Social Survey Division, HMSO.

MAUSS, Marcel (1923) 'Essai sur le don, forme archaïque de l'échange', *Année sociologique.* N.S. 1 (English translation: *The Gift: Forms and Functions of Exchange in Archaic Societies.* London: Cohen & West, 1954).

MEAD, Margaret (1943a) 'The factor of food habits', *Annals of the American Academy of Political and Social Science* 225: 136–41.

MEAD, Margaret (1943b) 'Dietary patterns and food habits', *Journal of the American Dietetic Association* 19(1): 1–5.

MEAD, Margaret (1949) 'Cultural patterning and nutritionally relevant behavior', *Journal of the American Dietetic Association* 25: 677–80.

MEAD, Margaret (1957) 'We don't like what we don't eat', *Cyprus Medical Journal* 9: 90–3.

MEAD, Margaret (1964) *Food Habits Research: Problems of the 1960s.* Washington DC: National Research Council.

MEAD, Margaret (1970) 'The changing significance of food', *American Scientist* 58: 176–81.

MEADOWS, G.N., R.L. PALMER, E.U.M. NEWBALL and J.M.T. KENRICK (1986) 'Eating attitudes and disorder in young women: a general practice based survey', *Psychological Medicine* 16: 351–57.

MEDLIK, S. (1972) *Profile of the Hotel and Catering Industry.* London: Heinemann.

MENNELL, Stephen (1985) *All Manners of Food: Eating and Taste in England and France from the Middle Ages to the Present.* Oxford: Basil Blackwell.

MENNELL, Stephen (1986a) 'Prospects for the history of food', *Groniek: Gronings Historisch Tijdschrift* 95: 7–21.

MENNELL, Stephen (1986b) 'Uber die Zivilisierung der Eßlust', *Zeitschrift für Soziologie* 15(6): 406–21.

MENNELL, Stephen (1987a) 'On the Civilising of Appetite', *Theory, Culture and Society* 4(3–4): 373–403.

MENNELL, Stephen (1987b) 'Eten in Nederland', *De Gids* 150(2–3): 199–207.

MENNELL, Stephen (1988) 'Indigestion in the nineteenth century: aspects of English taste and anxiety', pp. 153–61 in *Proceedings of the Seventh Oxford Symposium on Food and Cookery.* London: Prospect Books.

MENNELL, Stephen (1989) *Norbert Elias: Civilisation and the Human Self-Image.* Oxford: Basil Blackwell.

MENNELL, Stephen and Katherine SIMONS (1989) 'Die Soziologie der Bulimie', pp. 11–30 in A. KÄMMERER and Barbara KLINGENSPOR (eds), *Bulimie: Zum Verständnis einer geschlechtsspezifischen Eßstörung.* Stuttgart: Kohlhammer.

MESSER, Ellen (1981) 'Hot-cold classification: theoretical and practical implications of a Mexican study', *Social Science and Medicine* 15B: 133–45.

MESSER, Ellen (1984) 'Anthropological perspectives on diet', *Annual Review of Anthropology* 13: 205–49.

MESSER, Ellen (1989) 'Indian nutritionists and international nutritional standards', *Social Science and Medicine* 29(12): 1393–9.

MIDDLETON, C. (1974) 'Sexual inequality and stratification theory', in F. PARKIN (ed.), *The Social Analysis of Class Structure.* London: Tavistock.

MILES Doan R. and L. BISHARAT (1990) 'Female autonomy and child nutritional status: the extended-family residential unit in Amman, Jordan', *Social Science and Medicine* 31(7): 783–9.

MILIO, N. (1981) 'Promoting Health through Structural Change: Analysis of the Origins and Implementation of Norways Farm-Food-Nutrition Policy', *Social Science and Medicine* 15A: 721–34.

MILIO, N. (1991) *Health for all policy in Finland*. Copenhagen: World Health Organisation.

MILLSTONE, Erik (1986) *Food additives: Taking the Lid off What we Really Eat*. Harmondsworth: Penguin.

MINTZ, Sidney W. (1985) *Sweetness and Power: The Place of Sugar in Modern History*. New York: Viking.

MINTZ, Sidney W. (1991) 'Color, taste and purity: some speculations on the meanings of marzipan', *Etnofoor* 4(1): 103–8.

MINUCHIN, S. (1978) *Psychosomatic Families: Anorexia Nervosa in Context*. Cambridge MA: Harvard University Press.

MOON, G. and L. TWIGG (1988) 'Health education and baseline data: issues and strategies in nutrition campaigning', *Social Science and Medicine* 26(1): 173–8.

MOORE, Henrietta L. (1990) 'When is a famine not a famine?', *Anthropology Today* 6(1): 1–3.

MORRIS, Lydia (1990) *The Workings of the Household*. Cambridge: Polity Press.

MURCOTT, Anne. (1982) 'On the social significance of the "cooked dinner" in South Wales', *Social Science Information* 21(4/5) 677–95.

MURCOTT, Anne (ed.) (1983a) *The Sociology of Food and Eating*. Aldershot. Gower.

MURCOTT, Anne (1983b) 'Cooking and the cooked: a note on the domestic preparation of meals', pp. 178–93 in A. MURCOTT, (ed.).

MURCOTT, Anne (1983c) 'Women's place: cookbooks' images of technique and technology in the British kitchen', *Women's Studies International Forum* 6 (1): 33–9.

MURCOTT, Anne (1983d) '"It's a pleasure to cook for him": food, mealtimes and gender in some South Wales households', in E. GARMARNIKOW et al. (eds), *The Public and the Private*. London: Heinemann.

MURCOTT, Anne (1986) 'Opening the "black box": food, eating and household relationships', *Socioaaliliaaketieteellinen aikakauslehti* (Journal of Social Medicine, Finland) Vuosikerta 2: 79–84.

MURCOTT, Anne (1987) 'Feeding the Children', *Journal of Education Policy* 2(3) 245–52.

MURCOTT, Anne (1988a) 'Sociological and social anthropological approaches to food and eating', *World Review of Nutrition and Diet* 55: 1–40.

MURCOTT, Anne (1988b) 'On the altered appetites of pregnancy', *Sociological Review* 36(4): 733–64.

MURCOTT, Anne (1988c) 'Meal-time myths hard to swallow', *Australian Financial Review* 14 December: 14.

MURCOTT, Anne (forthcoming a) 'Food and nutrition in post-war Britain', in P. CATERALL and J. OBELKEVIETCH (eds), *Understanding Post-War British Society* London: Routledge.

MURCOTT, Anne (forthcoming b) 'Purity and pollution: body management and the social place of infancy', in David MORGAN and Sue SCOTT (eds), *Body Matters: Readings in the Sociology of the Body*. Brighton: Falmer Press.

MURCOTT, Anne (forthcoming c) 'Talking of good food: an empirical study of women's conceptualisations', *Food and Foodways*.

MURDOCK, G.P. and C. PROVOST (1973) 'Factors in the division of labour by sex: a cross-cultural analysis', *Ethnology* XII(2): 203–25.

MYRDAL, A. and V. KLEIN (1968) *Women's Two Roles*. London: Routledge & Kegan Paul.

NASSER, Mervat (1988) 'Culture and weight consciousness', *Journal of Psychosomatic*

Research 32(6): 573–7.

NATIONAL FOOD AND NUTRITION BOARD (Netherlands) (1986) 'Richtlijnen goede voeding: een advies van de Voedingsraad' (Dietary Guidelines: Advice of the National Food and Nutrition Board) *Voeding (Netherlands Journal of Nutrition)* 47(6): 159–81.

NEWBY, H. (1983) 'Living from hand to mouth: the farmworker, food and agribusiness', in Anne MURCOTT (ed.).

NEWMAN, N.F. et al. (eds) (1990) *Hunger in History: Food Shortage, Poverty and Deprivation.* Oxford: Blackwell.

NICHTER, Mark (1985) 'Drink boiled water: a cultural analysis of a health education message', *Social Science and Medicine* 21(6): 667–9.

OAKLEY, A. (1974a) *Housewife.* Harmondsworth: Penguin.

OAKLEY, A. (1974b) *The Sociology of Housework.* London: Martin Robertson.

OBREGÓN, E. de (1985) 'L'Hambre en España' (Hunger in Spain), *Historia y Vida* 18 (204): 50–67.

ODEBIYI, A.I. (1989) 'Food taboos in maternal and child health: the views of traditional healers in Ile-Ife, Nigeria', *Social Science and Medicine* 28(9): 985–96.

ODDY, D.J. and D.S. MILLER (eds) (1976) *The Making of the Modern British Diet.* London: Croom Helm.

OKELY, Judith (1983) *The Traveller-Gypsies.* Cambridge: Cambridge University Press.

O'LAUGHLIN, B. (1974) 'Mediation of contradiction: why Mbum women do not eat chicken', in M.Z. ROSALDO and L. LAMPHERE (eds), *Women, Culture and Society.* Stanford: Stanford University Press.

ORBACH, M. (1977) *Hunters, Seamen and Entrepreneurs: the tuna senermen of San Diego.* Berkeley: University of California Press.

ORBACH, Susie (1978) *Fat is a Feminist Issue.* London: Paddington Press.

ORBACH, Susie (1986) *Hunger Strike.* London: Faber & Faber.

ORWELL, George (1974 [orig. 1933]) *Down and Out in Paris and London.* Harmondsworth: Penguin.

ORY, Pascale (1986) 'La France des gastronomes', *Histoire* 85: 89–93.

PAHL, Jan (1980) 'Patterns of money management within marriage', *Journal of Social Policy* 9(3): 313–35.

PAHL, Jan (1982) 'The allocation of money and the structuring of inequality within marriage', Board of Studies in Social Policy and Administration, University of Kent, mimeo.

PAHL, Jan (1989) *Money and Marriage.* London: Macmillan.

PAHL, R.E. (1984) *Divisions of Labour.* Oxford: Blackwell.

PALAZOLLI, M.S. (1974) *Self-Starvation: From the Intrapsychic to the Interpersonal Approach to Anorexia Nervosa.* London: Human Context Books.

PATERSON, E. (1981) 'Food-work: maids in a hospital kitchen', in Paul ATKINSON and Christian HEATH (eds), *Medical Work: Routines and Realities.* Farnborough, Hants: Gower.

PAULUS, Ingeborg (1974) *The Search for Pure Food. A Sociology of Legislation in Britain.* London: Martin Robertson.

PELLING, Margaret (1986) 'Food policy in the early modern period: medical practitioners and others', paper presented to the *Society for the Social History of Medicine* conference on the History of Nutrition, Sheffield University, July.

PELTO, Gretel H. (1984) 'Intrahousehold food distribution patterns', pp. 285–93 in R. ALAN (ed.), *Malnutrition: Determinants and Consequences.* New York: Liss.

PELTO, Gretel H. (1987) 'Cultural issues in maternal and child health and nutrition', *Social Science and Medicine* 25(6): 553–9.

PELTO G.H. and P.J. PELTO (1983) 'Diet and Delocalisation: Dietary Changes since 1750', *Journal of Interdisciplinary History* 14(2): 507–23.

PELTO, Gretel H., Pertti J. PELTO and Ellen MESSER (1989) *Research Methods in Nutritional Anthropology*. Tokyo: The United Nations University.

PELTO, P.J. and G.H. PELTO (1983) 'Nutrition, health and culture', in D.L. ROMANUCCI-ROSS, E.E. MOERMAN and R. TANCREDI (eds), *The Anthropology of Medicine*. New York: Bergin.

PERLÈS, Cathérine (1979) 'Les origines de la cuisine', *Communications* 31: 4–14.

PETCHERS, M.K., J. CHOW and K. NORDISH (1989) 'Urban Emergency Food Center Clients. Characteristics, Coping Strategies and Needs', *Journal of Sociology and Social Welfare* 16(2): 195–203.

PETERSON, Yen and Laura D. BIRG (1988) 'Top Hat: the Chef as Creative Occupation', *Free Inquiry in Creative Sociology* 16(1): 67–72.

PFISTER, C. (1988) 'Hunger: ein interdisciplinäres Problemfeld' (Hunger, an Interdisciplinary Problem Field), *Archiv für Sozialgeschichte* 28: 382–90.

PIETTE, A. (1989) 'Folklore ou esthétique du brouillage', *Recherches sociologiques* 20(2): 177–90.

PILOWSKY, I. and N. SPENCE (1977) 'Ethnicity and Illness Behaviour', *Psychological Medicine* 7: 447–52.

PILL, R. (1983) 'An apple a day ... some reflections on working class mothers' views on food and health', pp. 117–28 in Anne MURCOTT, (ed.).

PILL, Roisin and Nigel C.H. STOTT (1982) 'Concepts of illness causation and responsibility: some preliminary data from a sample of working class mothers', *Social Science and Medicine* 16: 43–52.

PILLSBURY, Richard (1990) *From Boarding House to Bistro: the American Restaurant Then and Now*. Boston: Unwin Hyman.

PITTE, Jean-Robert (1991) *Gastronomie française: histoire et géographie d'une passion*. Paris: Fayard.

PLATT, B.S. et al. (1963) *Food in Hospitals: a Study of Feeding Arrangements and the Nutritional Value of Meals in Hospitals*. London: Oxford University Press.

PLATT, J. (1969) 'Some problems in measuring the jointness of conjugal role-relationships', *Sociology* 3(3) 287–297.

POLIVY, J. and C.P. HERMAN (1987) 'Diagnosis and treatment of normal eating', *Journal of Consulting and Clinical Psychology*. 55: 635–44.

POLLERT, A. (1981) *Girls, Wives, Factory Lives*. London: Macmillan.

POLLOCK, K. (1988) 'On the nature of social stress: production of a modern mythology', *Social Science and Medicine* 26: 381–92.

POPKIN, Barry M. and Marisol LIM-YBANEZ (1982) 'Nutrition and school achievement', *Social Science and Medicine* 16: 53–61.

POSNER, T. (1983) 'The sweet things in life: aspects of the management of diabetic diet', in Anne MURCOTT (ed.).

POST, J.D. (1985) *Food Shortage, Climatic Variability, and Epidemic Disease in Pre-industrial Europe: The Mortality Rate in the Early 1740s*. Ithaca, Cornell University Press.

PRÄTTÄLÄ, Ritva (1989) 'Young people and food: socio-cultural studies of food consumption patterns', unpublished doctoral thesis, University of Helsinki.

PRÄTTÄLÄ, Ritva (1991) 'Outlining multidisciplinary food research', in Elisabeth L.

FURST et al. (eds), *Palatable Worlds: Sociocultural Food Studies*. Oslo: Solum.

PRÄTTÄLÄ, Ritva and Paivi HELMINEN (1990) 'Finnish meal patterns' in J.C. SOMOGYI and E.H. KOSKINEN (eds), *Nutritional Adaptation to New Life-Styles*. Basel: Karger.

PRESS, Irwin (1979) *The City as Context*. Illinois: University of Illinois Press.

PRIESTLAND, Gerald (1972) *Frying Tonight: The Saga of Fish and Chips*. London: Gentry Books.

PULLAR, Philippa (1970) *Consuming Passions*. London: Hamish Hamilton.

PYKE, Magnus (1970) *Food Science and Technology*. London: John Murray.

PYKE, Magnus (1972) *Technological Eating, Or Where does the Fish Finger Point?* London: John Murray.

PYNSON, Pascale (1989) *La France à Table, 1960–86*. Paris: Belfond.

RAMA, R. (1985) 'Do transnational agribusiness firms encourage the culture of developing countries? The Mexican experience', *International Social Science Journal* 37(3): 331–44.

REES, Teresa (forthcoming) *Women and the Labour Market*. London: Routledge.

REEVES, Maude Pember (1913) *Round About a Pound a Week*. London: G. Bell.

REITER, Ester (1991) *Making Fast Food: From the Frying Pan to the Fryer*. Montreal: McGill–Queens University Press.

RICHARDS, Audrey (1932) *Hunger and Work in a Savage Tribe: A Functional Study of Nutrition among the Southern Bantu*. London: Routledge.

RICHARDS, Audrey (1937) *The Food and Nutrition of African Natives*. London: International Institute of African Languages and Cultures.

RICHARDS, Audrey (1939) *Land, Labour and Diet in Northern Rhodesia*. Oxford: Oxford University Press.

RICHARDS, Audrey and E.M. WIDDOWSON (1936) 'A dietary study in northeastern Rhodesia', *Africa* 9: 166–96.

RIESMAN, David, with Nathan GLAZER and Reuel DENNEY (1961 [orig. 1950]) *The Lonely Crowd*. New Haven: Yale University Press.

RISSANEN, A. et al. (1988) 'Overweight and anthropometric changes in adulthood: a prospective study of 17,000 Finns', *International Journal of Obesity* 12: 391–401.

RITENBAUGH, Cheryl (1982) 'Obesity as a culture-bound syndrome', *Culture, Medicine and Psychiatry* 6: 347–61.

RIZVI, Najma (1991) 'Socioeconomic and cultural factors affecting interhousehold and intrahousehold food distribution in rural and urban Bangladesh', in Anne Sharman et al. (eds) *Diet and Domestic Life in Society*. Philadelphia: Temple Press.

ROBERTSON SMITH W. (1889) *The Religion of the Semites*. Edinburgh: Black.

ROBSON, J.R.K. (ed.), (1980) *Food, Ecology and Culture: Readings in the Anthropology of Dietary Practices*. New York: London: Gordon and Breach Science Publishers.

ROTBERG, Robert I. and Theodore K. RABB (eds) (1985) *Hunger and History. The Impact of Changing Food Production and Consumption Patterns on Society*. Cambridge: Cambridge University Press.

ROTH, J.A. (1963) *Timetables: structuring the passage of time in hospital treatment and other careers*. Indianapolis: Bobbs-Merrill.

ROTH, Julius A. (1976) *Health Purifiers and their Enemies*. London: Croom Helm.

ROTENBERG, R. (1981) 'The impact of industrialisation on meal patterns in Vienna, Austria', *Ecology of Food and Nutrition* 11: 25–35.

ROWNTREE, B. Seebohm (1901) *Poverty: A Study of Town Life*. London: Macmillan.

RUIVENKAMP, G. (1987) 'The social impacts of biotechnology on agriculture and Food Processing', *Development* 4: 58–9.

RUSSELL, G.F.M. (1979) 'Bulimia nervosa: an ominous variant of anorexia nervosa', *Psychological Medicine* 9: 429–48.

RUSSELL, H. (1984) '"Canadian ways": an introduction to comparative studies of housework, stoves and diet in Great Britain and Canada', *Material History Bulletin* 19: 1–12.

SALAMAN, R.N. (1949) *The History and Social Influence of the Potato*. Cambridge: Cambridge University Press (rev. edn 1985).

SCHROEDL, Alan (1972) 'The dish ran away with the spoon: ethnography of kitchen culture', in J.P. SPRADLEY and D.W. McCURDY (eds), *The Cultural Experience: ethnography in complex society*. Chicago: Science Research Associates.

SCHWARTZ, Donald M., Michael G. THOMPSON, and Craig L. JOHNSON (1982), 'Anorexia Nervosa and Bulimia: the sociocultural context', *International Journal of Eating Disorders* 1: 20–36 (reprinted in S. WILEY EMMETT (ed.), *Theory and Treatment of Anorexia Nervosa and Bulimia: Biomedical, Sociocultural and Pscyhological Perspectives*. New York: Brunner/Mazel Publishers, 1985).

SCHWARZ-COWAN, R. (1983) *More Work for Mother: The Ironies of Household Technology from the Open Hearth to the Microwave*. New York: Basic Books.

SCRIMSHAW, Nevin S. (1983) 'The value of contemporary food and nutrition studies for historians', *Journal of Interdisciplinary History* 14(2): 529–34.

SELLERBERG, A.M. (1991a) 'In food we trust: vitally necessary confidence – and unfamiliar ways of attaining it', in E. FURST et al. (eds), *Palatable Worlds: Sociocultural Food Studies*. Oslo: Solum.

SELLERBERG, A.M. (1991b) 'Expressivity within a time schedule: subordinated interaction on geriatric wards', *Sociology of Health & Illness* 13(1): 68–82.

SEN, Amartya K. (1981) *Poverty and Famines: An Essay on Entitlement and Deprivation*. Oxford: Oxford University Press.

SEN, Amartya K. (1985) *Women, Technology and Sexual Divisions*. Geneva: United Nations. (UNCTAD TT/79).

SEN, Amartya K. (1990) 'Food entitlement and economic chains', in Lucille F. Newman and William Crossgrove et al. (associate eds) *Hunger in History: Food Shortage, Poverty and Deprivation*, pp. 374–85.

SHACK, K.W., L.E. GRIVETTI and K.G.DEWEY (1990) 'Cash Cropping, Subsistence Agriculture and Nutritional Status among Mothers and Children in Lowland Papua New Guinea', *Social Science and Medicine* 31(1): 61–8.

SHAPIRO, Laura (1986) *Perfection Salad: Women and Cooking at the Turn of the Century*. New York: Henry Holt.

SHARMAN, Anne et al. (eds) (1991) *Diet and Domestic Life in Society*. Philadelphia: Temple University Press.

SHARPE, S. (1976) *'Just Like a Girl': how girls learn to be women*, Harmondsworth: Penguin.

SHEPHERD, R. (1990) 'Overview of factors influencing food choice', pp. 12–30 in M. ASHWELL (ed.), *Why we Eat What we Eat*. London: British Nutrition Foundation.

SHIFFLETT, Peggy A. and W. Alex McIntosh (1986) 'Food habits and future time: an exploratory study of age-appropriate food habits among the elderly', *International Journal of Aging and Human Development* 24(1): 1–15.

SIMMEL, Georg (1910) 'Soziologie der Mahlzeit', *Der Zeitgeist*. Supplement to *Berliner Tageblatt*. 19 October 1910. Reprinted in G. SIMMEL, *Brüche und Tür*.

Stuttgart, K.F. Köhler 1957, pp. 243–50 (English translation in Appendix, pp. 328–34, to Michael SYMONS, *Eating into Thinking: Explorations in the Sociology of Cuisine*. unpublished PhD thesis, Flinders University of South Australia, 1991).

SIMONS, Katherine (1990) 'Food Preferences and Compliance with Dietary Advice', upublished PhD thesis, University of Exeter.

SIMOONS, Frederick J. (1961) *Eat Not This Flesh: Food Avoidances in the Old World*. Madison: University of Wisconsin Press.

SMITH, Martin J. (1991) 'From policy community to issue network: *salmonella* in eggs and the new politics of food', *Public Administration* 69(Summer): 235–55.

SMITH, R.E.F. and David CHRISTIAN (1984) *Bread and Salt: A Social and Economic History of Food and Drink in Russia*. Cambridge: Cambridge University Press.

SMITH, Stephen L.J. (1985) 'Location patterns of urban restaurants', *Annals of Tourism Research* 12(4):581–602.

SORJ, Nernardo and John WILKINSON (1985) 'Modern food technology: industrialising nature', *International Social Science Journal* 37(3): 301–14.

SOROKIN, Pitirim A. (1975 [orig. 1922]) *Hunger as a Factor in Human Affairs*. Gainesville: University Presses of Florida.

SPENCER, Herbert (1898–1900) *The Principles of Sociology*. 3rd ed., 2 vols. in 5 parts, New York: D. Appleton.

SPRING RICE, Margery (1939) *Working-Class Wives: Their Health and Conditions*. Harmondsworth: Penguin.

STACEY, M. (1981) 'The division of labour revisited, or overcoming the two Adams', in P. ABRAMS et al. (eds), *Practice and Progress: British Sociology 1950–1980* London: Allen & Unwin.

STAHL, Ann Brower (1984) 'Hominid dietary selection before fire', *Current Anthropology* 25(2): 151–68.

STARR SERED, S. (1988) 'Food and holiness: cooking as a sacred act among middle eastern Jewish women', *Anthropological Quarterly* 61(3): 129–39.

STOUFF, Louis (1970) *Ravitaillement et alimentation en Provence aux 14ᵉ et 15ᵉ siècles*. Paris: Mouton.

STRASSER, S. (1982) *Never Done: A History of American Housework*. New York: Pantheon Books.

STRIEGEL-MOORE, R.H., L.R. SILBERSTEIN and J. RODIN (1986) 'Toward an understanding of risk factors for bulimia', *American Psychologist* 41: 246–63.

STUYVENBERG, J.H. (1969) *Margarine: An Economic, Social and Scientific History, 1869–1969*. Liverpool: Liverpool University Press.

SUKKARY-STOLBA, S. (1987) 'Food classification and the diets of young children in rural Egypt', *Social Science and Medicine* 25(4): 401–4.

SULER, John and Elaine BARTHOLOMEW (1986) 'The ideology of Overeaters Anonymous', *Social Policy* 16(4): 48–53.

SUPER, J.C. and T.C. WRIGHT (eds) (1985) *Food, Politics and Society in Latin America*. Lincoln: University of Nebraska Press.

SWANTZ, M.L. (1975) 'Socioeconomic causes of malnutrition in Moshi District'. Research Paper No. 38, Bureau of Resource Assessment and Land Use Planning, University of Dar es Salaam, Tanzania.

SWARTZ, Leslie (1987) 'Illness negotiation: the case of eating disorders', *Social Science and Medicine* 24(7): 613–618.

SYMONS, Michael (1982) *One Continuous Picnic: A History of Eating in Australia*. Adelaide: Duck Press.

SYMONS, Michael (1983) 'An "abominable" cuisine', *Petits Propos Culinaires* 15: 34–9.

TAN, Swe Poh (1982) 'Food ideology and food habits of Chinese immigrants in London and the growth of their young children', Department of Human Nutrition, London School of Hygiene and Tropical Medicine, mimeo.

TANNAHILL, R. (1973) *Food in History*. London: Eyre Methuen.

TEUTEBERG, H.-J. (1977) 'The beginnings of the modern milk age in Germany', pp. 283–312 in A. FENTON and T.M. OWEN (eds).

TEUTEBERG, H.-J. (1986) 'Periods and turning points in the history of European diet: a preliminary outline of problems and methods', pp. 11–23 in A. FENTON and E. KISBÁN (eds).

TEUTEBERG H.-J. (1987) 'Zum Problemfeld Urbanisierung und Ernährung in 19. Jahrhundert', in H. J. TEUTEBERG (ed.), *Durchbruch zum modernen Massenkonums. Lebensmittelmärkte und Lebensmittelqualität im Städtewachstum des Industriezeitalters*. Münster: Coppenrath Verlag.

TEUTEBERG, H.-J. and G. WIEGELMANN (1972) *Der Wandel der Nahrungs-gewohnheiten unter dem Einfluß der Industrialisierung*. Göttingen: Vandenhoeck und Ruprecht.

TEUTEBERG, H.-J. and G. WIEGELMANN (1986) *Unsere tägliche Kost: Geschichte und regionale Prägung*. Münster: Coppenrath Verlag.

THEODORATUS, R.J. (1977) 'Greek immigrant cuisines in America: continuity and change', pp. 313–23 in A. FENTON and T. M. OWEN (eds).

THEODORATUS, R.J. (1983) 'The changing patterns of Greek foodways in America', pp. 87–104 in A. DAVIDSON (ed.).

THOMAS, Graham and Christine ZMROCZEK (1985) 'Household technology: the "liberation" of women from the home?', in Paul CLOSE and Rosemary COLLINS (eds), *Family and Economy in Modern Society*. London: Macmillan.

THOMAS, G.C. (1981) 'The social background of childhood nutrition in the Ciskei', *Social Science and Medicine* 15A: 551–55.

THOMAS, J.E. (1979) 'The relation between knowledge about food and nutrition and food choice', in M. TURNER (ed.).

THOMAS, J.E. (1982) 'Food habits of the majority: evolution of the current U.K. pattern', *Proceedings of the Nutrition Society* 41: 211.

THOROGOOD, Nicki (1986) 'Race, class and gender: the politics of housework', London: unpublished paper.

THUILLIER, Guy (1979 [orig. 1968]) 'Water supplies in nineteenth-century Nivernais', pp. 109–25 in R. FORSTER and O. RANUM (eds).

TILLY, Louise A. (1985) 'Food entitlement, famine and conflict', pp. 135–51 in: R.I. ROTBERG and T.K. RABB (eds).

TINKER, Irene (1987) 'Street foods: testing assumptions about informal sector activity by women and men', *Current Sociology* 35(3).

TOLKSDORF, U. (1977) 'Development and decline of preferences and taboos in matters of food and drink', in A. FENTON and T.M. OWEN (eds).

TOLSON, A. (1977) *The Limits of Masculinity*. London: Tavistock.

TOMLINSON, Graham (1986) 'Thought for food: a study of written instructions', *Symbolic Interaction* 9(2): 201–16.

TOMS OLSON, Joan (1979) 'Role conflict between housework and child care', *Sociology of Work and Occupations* 6(4): 430–56.

TOPALOV, A.M. (1987) 'Religion and health: the case of the dietietics of the Seventh

Day Adventists', *Social Compass* 24(4): 509–14.

TOWNSEND, Peter (1979) *Poverty in the United Kingdom*. Harmondsworth: Penguin.

TOWNSEND, Peter and Nick DAVIDSON (1988) *Inequalities in Health: The Black Report*. Harmondsworth: Penguin.

TRUSWELL, A. Stewart and Ian DARNTON-HILL (1981) 'Food habits of adolescents', *Nutrition Reviews* 39(2): 73–88.

TUCKER, Katherine and Diva SANJUR (1988) 'Maternal employment and child nutrition in Panama', *Social Science and Medicine* 26(6): 605–12.

TURNER, Bryan S. (1982a) 'The discourse of diet', *Theory, Culture and Society* 1(1): 23–32.

TURNER, Bryan S. (1982b) 'The government of the body: medical regimens and the rationalisation of diet', *British Journal of Sociology* 33(2): 254–69.

TURNER, Bryan S. (1990) 'The talking disease: Hilda Bruch and anorexia nervosa', *Australian and New Zealand Journal of Sociology* 26(2): 157–69.

TURNER, Bryan S. (1991) 'patriarchy and anorexia nervosa: a reply to Jan Horsfall', *Australian and New Zealand Journal of Sociology* 27(2): 235–8.

TURNER, C. (1967) 'Conjugal roles and social networks: a re-examination of an hypothesis', *Human Relations* 20(2): 121–30.

TURNER, M. (ed.) (1979) *Nutrition and Lifestyles*. London: Applied Science Publishers.

TWIGG, Julia (1979) 'Food for thought: purity and vegetarianism', *Religion* 9(Spring) 13–35.

TWIGG, Julia (1983) 'Vegetarianism and the meanings of meat' in Anne MURCOTT (ed.).

UNDERWOOD, Peter and Barrie MARGETTS (1987) 'Cultural change, growth and feeding of children in an isolated rural region of Yemen', *Social Science and Medicine* 25(1): 1–7.

VALADEZ, J.J. and R. CLIGNET (1984) 'Household work as an ordeal: culture of standards versus standardization', *American Journal of Sociology* 89(4): 812–35.

VAN OTTERLOO, A.H. (1987) 'Foreign immigrants and the Dutch at table: 1945–1985. Bridging or widening the gap?', *Netherlands Journal of Sociology* 23(2): 126–43.

VAN OTTERLOO, A.H. (1990) *Eten en eetlust in Nederland 1840–1990. Een historisch-sociologische studie*. Amsterdam: Bert Bakker.

VAN OTTERLOO, A.H. and J. Van OGTROP (1989) *The regime of plenty, fat and sweet: talking with mothers on food and health*. Amsterdam: VU-Uitgeverij.

VAN DEN BERGHE, Pierre L. (1984) 'Ethnic cuisine, culture in nature', *Ethnic and Racial Studies* 7(3): 387–97.

VEBLEN, Thorstein (1953 [orig. 1899]) *The Theory of the Leisure Class*. New York: Mentor.

VERGOPOULOS, K. (1985) 'The end of agribusiness or the emergence of biotechnology', *International Social Science Journal* 37(3): 285–99.

VIVIER, M. (1987) 'Le jardin, garde-manger et pharmacie', *Cahiers de sociologie-Economique et Culturelle,- Ethnopsychologie* 8 (December): 57–82.

VOSKUIL, J.J. (1983) 'De weg naar luilekkerland' (The road to the land of Cockaigne), *Bijdragen en Mededelingen betreffebde de Geschiedenis der Nederlanden* 95(3): 460–82.

VOSKUIL, J.J. (1988) 'Die Verbreitung von Kaffe und Tee in den Niederlanden' (The Diffusion of Coffee and Tea in the Netherlands), pp. 407–28 in N.A. BRINGÉUS et al. (eds), *Wandel der Volkskultur in Europa: Festschrift für Günter Wiegelmann zum 60 Geburtstag* (*Change in Folk Culture: Festschrift for Günter Wiegelmann on his Sixtieth Birthday*), 2 vols. Münster: Coppenrath Verlag.

WAJCMAN, J. (1981) 'Work and the family: who gets "the best of both worlds"?' in CAMBRIDGE WOMEN'S STUDIES GROUP (eds), *Women in Society*. London: Virago.

WALLMAN, S. (1984) *Eight London Households*. London: Tavistock.

WARDLE, J. and H. BEINART (1981) 'Binge eating: a theoretical review', *British Journal of Clinical Psychology* 20: 97–109.

WATKINS, S.C. and J. MENKEN (1985) 'Famines in historical perspective', *Population and Development Review* 11(4): 647–75.

WEATHERILL, Lorna (1988) *Consumer Behaviour and Material Culture in Britain 1660–1760*. London: Routledge.

WEBER, Max (1976 [orig. 1909]) *The Agrarian Sociology of Ancient Civilisations*. London: New Left Books.

WELLIN, Edward (1955) 'Water boiling in a Peruvian town', in Benjamin PAUL (ed.), *Health, Culture and Community*. New York: Russell Sage Foundation.

WELSHMAN, John (1986) 'School meals and the problem of malnutrition in England and Wales 1900–1939', paper presented to Conference on Nutrition in History, Society for the Social History of Medicine, University of Sheffield, UK.

WENLOCK, R.W. et al. (1986) *The Diets of British Schoolchildren: preliminary report of a nutritional analysis of a nationwide dietary survey of British Schoolchildren*. London: HMSO.

WEST, J. (1980) 'A political economy of the family in capitalism: women, reproduction and wage labour' in T. NICHOLS (ed.), *Capital and Labour: a Marxist Primer*. Glasgow: Fontana.

WEST, J. (ed.) (1982) *Work, Women and the Labour Market*. London: Routledge & Kegan Paul.

WHEATON, Barbara Ketcham (1984) *Savouring the Past: The French Kitchen and Table from 1300 to 1789*. London: Chatto & Windus.

WHEELER, E. and Swee Poh TAN (1983) 'Food for equilibrium: the dietary principles and practice of Chinese families in London', in A. MURCOTT (ed.).

WHIT, William C. (1988) 'The politics of food', *Humanity and Society* 12 (3): 303–5.

WHIT, William C. (1990) 'The meaning of the health food movement'. Paper presented at the World Congress of Sociology, Madrid, July.

WHITEHEAD, Anne (1981) '"I'm hungry, mum": the politics of domestic budgeting', in Kate YOUNG, Carolyn WOLKOWITZ and Roslyn McCULLAGH (eds), *Of Marriage and the Market: Women's Subordination in International Perspective*. London: CSE Books.

WHITEHEAD, Margaret (1988) *Inequalities in Health: the Health Divide*, Harmondsworth; Penguin.

WHO (World Health Organisation) (1990) *Diet, Nutrition and the Prevention of Chronic Diseases*. Technical Report Series 797. Geneva: World Health Organisation.

WHYTE, William Foote (1946) 'When workers and customers meet', in W.F. Whyte (ed.), *Industry and Society*. New York: McGraw Hill.

WHYTE, William Foote (1948) *Human Relations in the Restaurant Industry*. New York: McGraw-Hill.

WHYTE, William Foote (1949) 'The social structure of the restaurant', *American Journal of Sociology* 54( ): 302–10.

WIEGELMANN, G. (1967) *Alltags und Festspeisen: Wandel und gegenwärtige Stellung*

(*Everyday and Festive Dishes, Change and Contemporary Position*), Marburg: N.G. Elwert.

WIEGELMANN, G. (1975) 'Ideen zu einer kartographischen Erfassung Europäischer Kostunterschiede' (Ideas on a Description of Differences in European Diet through Mapping), in N. VALONEN, J.U.E. LEHTONEN (eds), *Ethnologische Nahrungsforschung* (*Reports from the Second International Symposion for Ethnological Food Research*). Helsinki.

WILLI, J. and S. GROSSMAN (1983) 'Epidemiology of anorexia nervosa in a defined region of Switzerland', *American Journal of Psychiatry* 140: 564–7.

WILLIAMS, R. (1983) 'Concepts of health: an analysis of lay logic', *Sociology* 17: 185–205.

WILLIAMS, W.M. (1956) *The Sociology of an English Village: Gosforth*. London: Routledge & Kegan Paul.

WILMOTT, P. and M. YOUNG (1960) *Family and Class in a London Suburb*, Harmondsworth: Penguin.

WILSON, C. Anne (1973) *Food and Drink in Britain*. Harmondsworth: Penguin.

WILSON, C.S. (1979) 'Food, custom and nurture: an annotated bibliography on sociocultural and biocultural aspects of nutrition', *Journal of Nutrition Education* 11 (Supplement): 221–63.

WILSON, Charles (1954) *The History of Unilever: A Study in Economic Growth and Social Change*. 2 vols. London: Cassell.

WILSON, G. (1989) 'Family food systems: preventive health and dietary change – a policy to increase the health divide', *Journal of Social Policy* 18(2): 167–85.

WILSON, Monica (1972) 'The wedding cakes: a study of ritual change', in J.S. LA FONTAINE (ed.), *The Interpretation of Ritual*. London: Tavistock.

WINKLER, V. (1985) 'Markt, Norm und Staat, eine Rechts-und Marktsoziologische Fallstudie zur Situation vor Einführung der Schweizerische Lebensmittel-gesetzgebung', *Schweizerische Zeitschrift für Soziologie* 11(1): 91–110.

WOLF, Naomi (1990) *The Beauty Myth*. London: Chatto & Windus.

WOODHAM-SMITH, C. (1962) *The Great Hunger: Ireland 1845–9*. London: Hamish Hamilton.

WOODHAM-SMITH, C. (1975) 'The Great Hunger: Ireland, 1845–1849', in E. FORSTER and R. FORSTER (eds).

WOYS WEAVER, W. (1977) '*Die geschickte Hausfrau*: The first ethnic cookbook in the United States', pp. 343–64 in A. FENTON and T.M. OWEN (eds), *Food in Perspective: Proceedings of the Third International Conference on Ethnological Food Research*. Edinburgh: John Donald.

YOUNG, M. and P. WILMOTT (1957) *Family and Kinship in East London*, Harmondsworth: Penguin.

YOUNG, M. and P. WILMOTT (1975) *The Symmetrical Family*. Harmondsworth: Penguin.

YUDKIN, John and J.C. McKENZIE (1964) *Changing Food Habits*. London: MacGibbon & Kee.

ZACKON, D. (1970) 'Family food behaviour and attitudes', Department of Nutrition, Queen Elizabeth College, London: mimeo.

ZERUBAVEL, Eviatar (1979) *Patterns of Time in Hospital Life: A Sociological Perspective*. Chicago: Chicago University Press.

ZOLA, I.K. (1973) 'Pathways to the Doctor: from Person to Patient', *Social Science and Medicine* 7(9): 677–89.

Index

Abel, Wilhelm 62, 63
additives, food 71–2, 73
Africa 7, 20–2, 43, 78, 96, 110
agribusiness 72
alcohol 3, 55
Althusser, Louis 12
Anderson, Eugene N. 26, 43
Annales School 5–6, 24, 31–2
anorexia nervosa 5,17, 38, 46, 48–53
anthropology 1, 2, 6–7, 8–11, 15, 20–2,
  28–9, 32–4, 37
Appadurai, Arjun 118
appetite 17, 45, 48–9
aristocracy 23
Armelagos, George 127
Arnott, M. 28, 30
Aron, Jean-Paul, 24, 32
Atkinson, Paul A. 45
Australia 26, 38, 58, 76, 96
Aymard, Maurice 119

Barker, M.E. 54, 56
Barlösius, Eva 25, 73
Barthes, Roland 8, 11
Batstone, Eric 116
Baudrillard, Jean 84
Beardsworth, Alan 46, 119
beer 56
Beinart, H. 50
Belasco, W. J. 73–4
Berghe, Pierre van den 80, 115
biotechnology 71–2
Bisharat, L. 38
Blumer, Herbert 4
Bohemia 27
books, cookery 88, 90, 95
Boserup, Esther 64
Boskind-Lohdahl, M. 52–3
Bott, Elizabeth 96
Bourdieu, Pierre 3, 11–12, 13, 24, 56–7,
  67, 92, 119
Braudel, Fernand 5–6, 24, 31, 62, 63, 76
Brewer, Stella 14
Brillat-Savarin, J.-A. 84
Bringéus, Nils-Arvid 31
Bruch, Hilde 50, 52, 53

Brumberg, Joan J. 48
Buddhism 16
bulimia 5, 17, 38, 46, 48–53
Burnett, John 23, 30, 35, 62, 116

cafés *see* coffee houses
Calnan, M. 55
Calvo, M. 79, 80
Canada 104
caste system 15–16
Castillero-Calvo, Alfredo 76
Chang, Kwang-chi 26, 32
Chapman, Malcolm 55–56
Charles, Nickie 45, 57, 91–2, 100, 106–10
chefs *see* cooks, professional
Chermin, Kim 53
Cheyne, George 49
China 21, 26, 33, 43
Chivers, T. S. 87
Christian, David 27
coffee 29, 30, 32, 55, 82
coffee houses 82
colonialism 75–80
commensality 115–18
consumption, conspicuous 2–3
cookery, domestic 22, 24–5 88–94,
  95–111
cooks
  female 22, 96
  male 22, 25, 96
  professional 81, 83, 85–7, 96
courtiers 22–3, 24
Crawford, Sir William 70
Crotty, P. A. 112, 113
cuisine
  haute 22–3, 26
  nouvelle 24
culture 5, 9, 13, 14, 20, 31
Curnonsky 84

Dambinska, M. 31
Davidson, Alan 76
Davison, C. 42
Dawell, F. 76–7
Delphy, C. 104
Denmark 54, 69
DeVault, Marjorie L. 102, 109